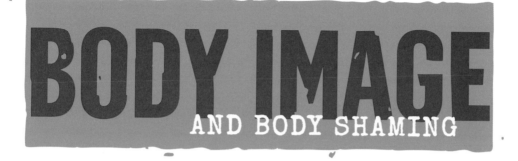

BODY IMAGE
AND BODY SHAMING

WITHDRAWN

By Meghan Green

Portions of this book originally appeared in *Body Image* by Robert D. Lankford, Jr.

LUCENT
PRESS

Published in 2017 by
Lucent Press, an Imprint of Greenhaven Publishing, LLC
353 3rd Avenue
Suite 255
New York, NY 10010

Designer: Andrea Davison-Bartolotta
Editor: Jennifer Lombardo

Cataloging-in-Publication Data

Names: Green, Meghan.
Title: Body image and body shaming / Meghan Green.
Description: New York : Lucent Press, 2017. | Series: Hot topics| Includes index.
Identifiers: ISBN 9781534560161 (library bound) | ISBN 9781534560130 (ebook)
Subjects: LCSH: Body image in children–Juvenile literature. | Body image–Juvenile literature. | Child psychology–Juvenile literature.
Classification: LCC BF723.B6 G74 2017 | DDC 306.4'613–dc23

Printed in the United States of America

CPSIA compliance information: Batch #CW17KL: For further information contact Greenhaven Publishing LLC, New York, New York at 1-844-317-7404.

Please visit our website, www.greenhavenpublishing.com. For a free color catalog of all our high-quality books, call toll free 1-844-317-7404 or fax 1-844-317-7405.

CONTENTS

FOREWORD 4

INTRODUCTION 6
The Emphasis on Appearance

CHAPTER 1 10
Understanding Body Image

CHAPTER 2 24
Body Image: Nature vs. Nurture

CHAPTER 3 41
The Role of Media in Shaping Body Image

CHAPTER 4 54
The Problem with Advertising

CHAPTER 5 65
Consequences of Poor Body Image

CHAPTER 6 80
Body Modifications

NOTES 91

DISCUSSION QUESTIONS 98

ORGANIZATIONS TO CONTACT 100

FOR MORE INFORMATION 102

INDEX 106

PICTURE CREDITS 111

ABOUT THE AUTHOR 112

Adolescence is a time when many people begin to take notice of the world around them. News channels, blogs, and talk radio shows are constantly promoting one view or another; very few are unbiased. Young people also hear conflicting information from parents, friends, teachers, and acquaintances. Often, they will hear only one side of an issue or be given flawed information. People who are trying to support a particular viewpoint may cite inaccurate facts and statistics on their blogs, and news programs present many conflicting views of important issues in our society. In a world where it seems everyone has a platform to share their thoughts, it can be difficult to find unbiased, accurate information about important issues.

It is not only facts that are important. In blog posts, in comments on online videos, and on talk shows, people will share opinions that are not necessarily true or false, but can still have a strong impact. For example, many young people struggle with their body image. Seeing or hearing negative comments about particular body types online can have a huge effect on the way someone views himself or herself and may lead to depression and anxiety. Although it is important not to keep information hidden from young people under the guise of protecting them, it is equally important to offer encouragement on issues that affect their mental health.

The titles in the Hot Topics series provide readers with different viewpoints on important issues in today's society. Many of these issues, such as teen pregnancy and Internet safety, are of immediate concern to young people. This series aims to give readers factual context on these crucial topics in a way that lets them form their own opinions. The facts presented throughout also serve to empower readers to help themselves or support people they know who are struggling with many of the challenges adolescents face today. Although negative viewpoints are not ignored or downplayed, this series allows young people to see that the challenges they face are not insurmountable. Eating disorders can be overcome, the Internet can be navigated safely, and pregnant teens do not have to feel hopeless.

Quotes encompassing all viewpoints are presented and cited so readers can trace them back to their original source, verifying for themselves whether the information comes from a reputable place. Additional books and websites are listed, giving readers a starting point from which to continue their own research. Chapter questions encourage discussion, allowing young people to hear and understand their classmates' points of view as they further solidify their own. Full-color photographs and enlightening charts provide a deeper understanding of the topics at hand. All of these features augment the informative text, helping young people understand the world they live in and formulate their own opinions concerning the best way they can improve it.

The Emphasis on Appearance

Since the early 1980s, body image has been at the center of public debate, generating much discussion and, at times, controversy. Simply defined, body image is the concept that each individual forms about his or her own appearance. In the public realm, however, ideas about body image have splintered into a broad array of issues with personal, social, and political implications. Weight, for instance, has become a hot-button issue. People can be shamed for either being too thin or too fat, and these standards are arbitrary, decided on mostly by people who feel that another person's body type is an insult to their own. This type of shaming occurs every day, both on the Internet and in the world at large, and it affects people of both sexes.

Issues surrounding body image include dieting, weight lifting, and eating disorders. Dieting has become a multibillion-dollar industry in the United States and around the world, as men and women attempt to achieve and maintain an ideal body weight. Likewise, membership in gyms and health clubs has become increasingly popular. Many people, however, rely on more extreme methods to control their body shapes. While statistics on eating disorders are difficult to verify, the American Psychological Association (APA) reports that anorexia, bulimia, and binge eating are all on the rise. Furthermore, while these diseases have been traditionally associated with women, men have begun developing these disorders in greater numbers.

While women may wish to become thinner, many men wish to become more muscular. In some cases, this has led to exercise addiction and steroid abuse.

Decorating and physically altering the body also fall under the umbrella of body image topics. Pierced ears, for instance, allow individuals to enhance that part of their body, potentially enhancing their overall body image. During the 1970s, body piercings and tattoos were frequently associated with social

Young girls and self-esteem

8 of 10

10-year-old girls in the United States have been on a diet

42% of girls in first through third grade want to be thinner

37% of those girls have already dieted

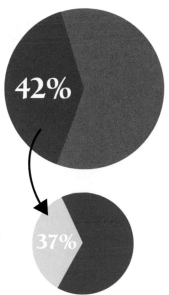

Weight is a major concern for young people, especially girls.

subgroups such as punk rockers. Body jewelry helped identify individuals as members of the punk community, working as a social shortcut while also separating them from the mainstream. Today, piercings and tattoos have become more fashionable. As they gain acceptance in mainstream society, more extreme forms of body modifications have sprung up that have not yet been accepted by the larger culture. These include dermal implants, tongue splitting, and corset piercings. Likewise, cosmetic surgery has become much more common, with millions of men and women receiving liposuction, Botox injections, and face-lifts every year. These changes suggest that men and women today have become more focused on body image issues and that, in some cases, it has become socially acceptable to alter or decorate the body in order to enhance one's body image. However, the range of activities that are considered socially acceptable is very narrow. Anything that falls outside of that norm is generally considered scary or disgusting by the majority of people and only accepted by social subgroups, which can lead to teasing or harassment.

Researchers believe that a number of factors—including genes, family, peers, the media, and advertising—influence the development of body image. Research also suggests that a number of other factors, including gender and age, also affect how men and women think about body image issues. The

Some people enjoy changing their appearance with multiple piercings.

development of body image, then, is a complex issue and one that researchers will continue to study closely.

Because body image has become a much-discussed and much-debated issue, some observers have suggested that it has become an obsession. This is reflected in a number of studies in Western cultures that suggest that body image is the single most important factor in a person's overall self-image. Body image is focused on physical appearance, but self-image is a broader concept that includes an individual's image of his or her over-all personality. By weighing body image so heavily, a person who thinks they are attractive will often have both a positive body image and a positive self-image. While most people wish to be considered attractive, the intense focus on body image may ignore many other aspects of an individual's personality. Whether or not one agrees that men and women have become too focused on body image in contemporary culture, the issues that have developed around body image will likely remain pressing ones.

CHAPTER 1

Understanding Body Image

Everyone has a different concept of the ideal body type. This can be seen in the way people feel about their own body as well as what they find attractive in others. For some, there is no ideal type—they find all bodies beautiful. Others have a very strict definition of what is acceptable. There is no one right answer to the question of what is the "perfect" body. It is important to note that preferences vary from person to person, and people who do not conform to one person's preference are not wrong or bad.

People's personal body image is shaped by several factors: how they feel about themselves, what their friends and family say about them, and what they see in the media. Standards of beauty vary from person to person and culture to culture, and they can change drastically over the course of history. For instance, in the past, it was considered a sign of wealth and privilege in the United States to be overweight. This is still true in some countries today, such as India, Mongolia, and some African nations.

No matter what the standards of beauty are in a society, there are always people who look down on those who do not meet those expectations. Creating a positive body image, regardless of what other people say, is extremely important because it not only affects how we feel about ourselves, but how we interact with others. Positive relationships are difficult to form when people feel bad about themselves, and self-image has a large impact on self-esteem.

Variations in Body Image

Everyone has a body image, and it is normal to want to be attractive. Body image, however, is a much broader concept than attractiveness. Body image is a person's perception of his or her own physical appearance and what that person believes other people think of it. This image includes physical attractiveness, but it also includes clothing and general presentation (hair, makeup, shoes, etc.). When people look in the mirror and ask "Am I attractive?" and "Will my friends like my new outfit?" they are considering their own body image. When people comment on the physical appearance of people they see in magazines, on billboards, and on television, they are judging others' body image.

An individual's concept of his or her own body image, however, does not always match his or her physical appearance. "Even though people say that 'the mirror doesn't lie,'" clinician Barbara Moe noted, "the mental picture we form about our bodies is often totally different from the actual appearances of our bodies."[1] It is common, for instance, for many individuals to believe that they weigh more than they do or that they are overweight when they are not. "Studies show that more than 60 percent of female high-school students believe they are overweight, when in fact less than 20 percent really are,"[2] social worker and author Diane Yancey concluded. The difference between these two images can lead to inner conflict, especially when an individual believes he or she is overweight, potentially influencing that person's overall self-assessment.

Feeling overweight can cause distress, even if the person is not actually overweight.

In many Western cultures, so much emphasis is placed on body image that it may seem to be the same thing as self-image. Self-image, however, is a broader concept that includes a person's physical, spiritual, and mental selves. Because physical appearance has become so important in contemporary culture, however, body image is frequently connected to self-esteem. "In industrialized cultures, body image, including perception of overall physical appearance, is probably the most important component of an adolescent's global self-esteem," observed psychologists Michael P. Levine and Linda Smolak. "The connection may be stronger during adolescence than in other age periods."[3] Concern over weight, height, and appearance may be normal, but it can also have a negative impact on adolescents if those traits do not match a person's idealized image.

Two Types of Body Image

Men and women develop both positive and negative body images. Generally, people with a positive body image are satisfied with their appearance and believe others also view them positively or do not let others' negative perceptions of them change their perception of themselves. The National Eating Disorders Association (NEDA) offers the following definition of a positive body image:

- *A clear, true perception of your shape—you see the various parts of your body as they really are.*

- *You celebrate and appreciate your natural body shape, and you understand that a person's physical appearance says very little about their character and value as a person.*

- *You feel proud and accepting of your unique body and refuse to spend an unreasonable amount of time worrying about food, weight, and calories.*

- *You feel comfortable and confident in your body.*[4]

Dissatisfaction with one's physical appearance can lead to a negative body image. A common example would be exces-

A positive body image can improve overall self-esteem.

sive worrying about gaining weight. Simply put, negative body image "means that no matter how our body looks to others, we don't think it looks good enough," clinical psychologist Joni E. Johnston explained. "If a teenager or adult believes themselves to be overweight and perceive[s] that the culture they live in considers an overweight person unattractive, then they may internalize a negative body image."[5] NEDA defines negative body image in the following way:

- *A distorted perception of your shape—you perceive parts of your body unlike they really are.*

- *You are convinced that only other people are attractive and that your body size or shape is a sign of personal failure.*

- *You feel ashamed, self-conscious, and anxious about your body.*

- *You feel uncomfortable and awkward in your body.*[6]

Cultural Changes in Body Image

The way we see our body has a lot to do with what our culture says is ideal, but these are not absolute truths; ideas about body image have changed frequently over time and will continue to change. Whether the issue is weight—who is considered thin and who is considered obese—or beauty—who is considered stunning and who is considered average—standards have continued to shift throughout time and across cultures.

People Are Hardest on Themselves

When considering body image, it is easy for most men and women to worry about what other people think. Still, the worst criticism is often self-criticism. Emily Starr, writing in the book *No Body's Perfect*, identified her worst critic:

It is often said that seeing is believing; yet when it comes to one's own reflection, I've never found that statement to possess any truth. In fact, hearing is often believing. There was once this girl, and every day when she saw me she would sneer and say, "You're hideous." "You're fat." "Your complexion is horrible." "Your outfit looks stupid." She said these things over and over again till I just buried my head in my hands and sobbed uncontrollably every time I saw my own reflection. She was right, I told myself. She was right about everything. The words were constantly echoing in my mind, ringing in my ears, screaming in my face. And that girl wasn't a bully at school or an enemy on the soccer field. She didn't have a crush on my boyfriend or any reason to hate me with so much passion. She was me. My tormentor was myself.[1]

1. Quoted in Kimberly Kirberger, *No Body's Perfect: Stories by Teens About Body Image, Self-Acceptance, and the Search for Identity.* New York, NY: Scholastic, 2003, p. 75.

Researchers have many theories about why weight and beauty standards change. One popular theory suggests that ideal weight revolves around wealth and poverty. In Europe's past, a big body was often considered healthy and attractive because it

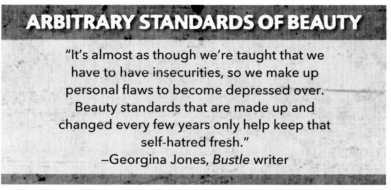

ARBITRARY STANDARDS OF BEAUTY

"It's almost as though we're taught that we have to have insecurities, so we make up personal flaws to become depressed over. Beauty standards that are made up and changed every few years only help keep that self-hatred fresh."

–Georgina Jones, *Bustle* writer

Georgina Jones, "Why Women's Ideal Body Shapes Throughout History Show How Arbitrary Beauty Standards Really Are," *Bustle*, September 29, 2015. www.bustle.com/articles/101630-why-womens-ideal-body-shapes-throughout-history-show-how-arbitrary-beauty-standards-really-are.

showed that someone had enough money to buy a lot of food and did not have to work—they could sit around all day. In contrast, a muscular body type was looked down on because it was a sign that someone was poor enough that he or she had to do manual labor. This is still the case in some countries around the world where people have to do hard work in order to survive. These views typically start to change when a country gains more overall wealth and starts to industrialize, meaning that there are more machines to do the hard labor, which gives even people who are less wealthy more leisure time. With women, healthiness also seemed to symbolize the ability to have children within traditional cultures. If men and women were overweight in traditional cultures, it was because they were prosperous. However, these kinds of perceptions are constantly shifting. Writing about prosperity in China a decade ago, Rachel Huxley and YangFeng Wu noted, "In Chinese culture, there is still a widespread belief that excess body fat represents health and prosperity. This may be a consequence of the famines and chronic malnutrition that caused millions of deaths in the past two centuries."[7] Today, the ideal throughout most of China, especially in city centers, has changed to an extremely thin body type and very white skin, which is based on Western fashion models. Skin-whitening products are commonly sold in drugstores, and many women will not go out in the sun without an umbrella to prevent them from getting a tan.

In wealthier countries such as the United States, where the majority of people can eat as much as they wish, body weight no longer represents prosperity. Thinness, sociologists have suggested, may now represent higher social status. Economics play a large part in this. Several studies suggest that junk food may be cheaper than healthy food, which means low-income people are generally more frequently overweight. Having less money to spend on food causes them to choose foods that are bad for their health but cost less and will fill them up. For example, they would be more likely to choose a $1 hamburger than $7 worth of fruit. The price of food depends on many factors, such as whether they are going to a restaurant or a grocery store, which stores they shop at, the quality of the food they are buying, the amount of food they are buying, and the area where they live.

Historically, opinions about weight and beauty have often been more focused on women than men. Various arguments have attempted to explain why this is true. One argument states that, because marriage was considered necessary for the upper-class and middle-class women who rarely worked and frequently could not inherit property, social pressure focused on women's attractiveness.

Middle-class and upper-class men, on the other hand, would have been more defined by their profession or wealth. Today, however, many social observers believe this focus is changing.

Beauty Standards Around the World

Many changes in how body image has been viewed are connected to cultural customs, such as the binding of feet in ancient China. Beginning around AD 1000, the upper classes in China believed that the practice of foot-binding enhanced women's beauty. "A pair of perfectly bound feet must meet seven qualifications—small, thin, pointed, arched, fragrant, soft, and straight—in order to become a piece of art,"[8] wrote author Wang Ping. Over time, the tradition of foot-binding became fashionable. The process of binding a woman's foot, however, was long and painful, requiring the displacement of the natural bone structure and wearing special shoes. Women with bound feet had limited mobility and took small steps. Perhaps the biggest irony of foot-binding was that it was difficult to keep a bound foot clean because of folds in the skin, allowing for the growth of fungi and producing an odor. However, it continued because society at the time told women that they would be ugly if they did not do it, and the pressure to be seen as beautiful outweighed practicality for many people. Wang Ping described her own experience with foot-binding from a third-person point of view in *Aching for Beauty: Footbinding in China*:

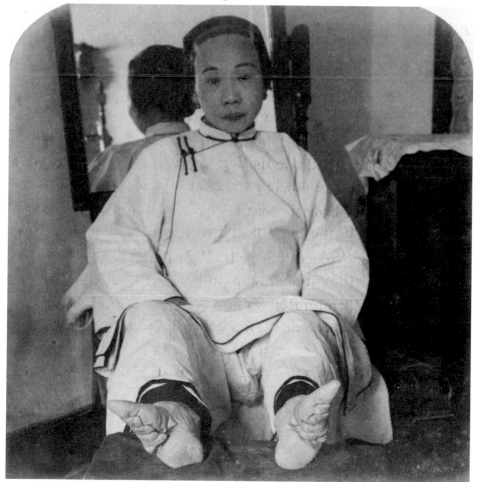

Foot-binding was a painful process that made women's feet look unnaturally small.

At the age of nine she began to bind her feet on her own. She did not know the elaborate method of the traditional footbinding ... She invented her own method of binding, wrapping her feet tightly with layers of elastic bands to prevent her feet from growing longer and wider. Though she did not bend her toes under her soles or break her bones, it still hurt. Her bandaged feet were on fire day and night. Each step felt as though she were walking on broken glass barefooted. But she bore the pain silently, and with much pride. She was determined to keep her feet from growing.[9]

The practice of foot-binding continued in China until the 1900s, when more modern people began to consider footbinding old-fashioned and snobby.

In other eras, tradition and custom influenced the development of body image in different ways. In Europe during the 1600s, for instance, many people considered plumpness to be pleasing. "Plumpness was considered fashionable ... until

Waist Training

Corsets were popular from the mid-16th to early 19th centuries as underclothing that made the waist look smaller, and they are starting to come back into fashion today. Celebrities, including Kim Kardashian and Jessica Alba, have promoted them as a weight-loss tool, saying that they make the waist smaller. However, doctors say this is untrue. Body fat around the waist will not disappear; it will just be pushed down so the waist looks smaller. Wearing a corset for short periods of time—two to four hours—can help improve posture, but wearing it for longer can bruise the skin. Also, lacing it too tightly can push the internal organs together. It can make taking deep breaths difficult, which limits any kind of physical activity, and it may make eating difficult as well. People could lose weight from eating smaller portions or because of how much they sweat when they wear a corset, but weight loss from these methods is easy to reverse without making long-term diet and exercise changes.

relatively recently,"[10] researcher Sarah Grogan has noted. This perspective is shown in the art of Peter Paul Rubens, a Flemish painter in the 1600s. The women who appeared in his paintings, including Rubens's wife Helene, were variously described as fleshy, plump, and voluptuous. "The women Rubens celebrated in his art," author Shari Graydon wrote, "boast dimpled thighs, ample arms, and ripples of fat around their bodies."[11] The women that Rubens painted for commissions were frequently wealthy and may have weighed more than women of the lower classes during the same time period.

As they did in Europe, ideals about body image also changed over time in the United States. Researcher Barbara A. Cohen wrote that women in colonial America (before 1776) were bigger

Thinness was not always the ideal body type throughout history, as this painting by Peter Paul Rubens shows.

and more muscular, and they were considered both attractive and healthy. She has said:

> This was a period of time in the history of our country in which size and strength were important assets for a woman to possess, for her own survival as well as her desirability as a wife, mother and worker of the land. Her fertility was important because the more children she could produce, the more free labor or helpers the family would have to work the land.[12]

Changes in the United States

Ideas about beauty shifted near the end of the 1800s in the United States. While traditions overlapped newer trends, the fashion industry and national magazines increasingly influenced body ideals. An early example of this influence was the craze for the Gibson girl in the United States between the 1890s and World War I (1917).

The Gibson Girl—drawn for magazines by illustrator Charles Dana Gibson—became the ideal for younger women. While she kept the hourglass figure of the ideal Victorian woman, her waist—held in by a corset—was slender. By exchanging frilly petticoats for a more practical blouse, the Gibson girl also revealed her figure. Energetic and on the go, she represented youthful enthusiasm and the changing roles for women within American society.

The wide circulation of these magazines also offered a new way for people to learn about trends in fashion. Previously, men and women were primarily influenced by the people in their communities, but the appearance of the Gibson girl in new magazines, such as *Ladies' Home Journal*, in the late 1800s helped spread these ideals nationally. "The Gibson girl swept the nation," noted Bob Batchelor in the book *The 1900s*. "Her image could be found everywhere, from pinups on college campuses to the Alaskan Klondike."[13]

Then came the neatly dressed Gibson man. With his hair slicked back and parted in the middle, combined with a square jaw and clean-shaven face, he was seen as the ideal companion for the Gibson girl. Like her, he represented a youthful idea that appealed to a younger generation. Both the Gibson girl and man also emphasized new, more open attitudes toward body image in the United States.

These social changes that allowed more choice in the public display of bodies in the United States—especially women's bodies—continued in the 1920s with flappers. Flappers wore short, straight dresses called shifts that de-emphasized women's hips and breasts while emphasizing bare legs (from the knees down) and bare arms. Flappers refused to wear the traditional corset that made them look curvy, and they rolled their stockings down to their knees in order to make dancing easier. They also rebelled against tradition by bobbing, or shortening, their hair. The flapper look was modern, and it represented freedom of movement, the growing number of women in the workplace, and changing ideas about sexuality.

The Role of Models in Body Image

A number of social observers pinpoint obsession with thinness to the mid-1960s in Britain and the United States and a trend that was symbolized by the appearance of a model named Twiggy. In 1966, the 16-year-old, single-named Twiggy became a supermodel in England, and she debuted in the United States the following year. "Twiggy was the forerunner of all waiflike, broomstick-thin models of today,"[14] authors Dorothy Hoobler and Thomas Hoobler wrote. She weighed 91 pounds (41.3 kg), and with small hips and no noticeable breasts, she represented an androgynous, or unisex, style. Many fashion designers found the new, thinner style the ideal form of youth and beauty to display current lines of clothing in *Cosmopolitan* and other women's magazines.

Other trends in fashion during the 1960s strengthened this new development of the thinner body style. Most noticeable among these was the popularity of the bikini in the 1960s.

Even if one body style remains more popular or noticeable at a particular time period, other styles continue to emerge.

A number of social observers have suggested that a new body style based on physical fitness has become America's "ideal" body type—the type most often seen in the media. "Now it is

Twiggy started the trend of very thin supermodels. Even today, models such as this woman continue to copy Twiggy's style.

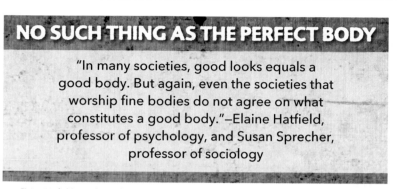

NO SUCH THING AS THE PERFECT BODY

"In many societies, good looks equals a
good body. But again, even the societies that
worship fine bodies do not agree on what
constitutes a good body."—Elaine Hatfield,
professor of psychology, and Susan Sprecher,
professor of sociology

Elaine Hatfield and Susan Sprecher. *Mirror, Mirror: The Importance of Looks in Everyday Life.*
Albany, NY: New York Press, 1986, p. 9.

muscle tone, skin tone, and 'being in shape,'"[15] author Hillel
Schwartz noted, rather than just being very skinny. Since the
1980s, Americans have seen the growth of the exercise industry, and today, millions of men and women have joined gyms.
This trend has also been supported by a greater awareness that
better eating habits and regular exercise could lead to a healthier
lifestyle. "In the '70s and '80s, we exercised and dieted excessively to achieve the Twiggy model image," wrote Gilda Marx
in *American Fitness.* "Now we know ultra-thinness is not
healthy"[16] when it is achieved by not eating enough combined
with exercising too much.

CHAPTER 2

Body Image:
Nature vs. Nurture

The way a person looks is mostly determined by his or her genetics. It can be very difficult to change things that are genetically determined. For instance, someone who comes from a family that is genetically predisposed to being overweight may have a lot of trouble losing weight, even with diet and exercise. Similarly, someone who comes from a very thin family may have a hard time gaining weight.

Genetics play a role in weight, but they are not the only factor.

People generally like some things about themselves and dislike others; it is rare for someone to either love or hate every single thing. One of the earliest influences on which things people like or dislike about their body comes from lessons children learn from parents, guardians, and siblings. These influences can also include friends at school and extended family members such as grandparents. Boys and girls will frequently learn their first lessons about body image from parents and guardians by watching their behavior or hearing how they speak about bodies. Adora Svitak, a columnist for the *Huffington Post* who is of Asian descent, has written about how badly she wanted to be white when she was younger: "I used to think that it was my problem, some strange fault I couldn't shake, and then I started thinking. I remembered relatives' comments on fair skin."[17] Another girl she interviewed spoke about the pressure for Asians to be thin: "When I came back from my first year of college in New York, my mother whispered to me, 'You're a little fat now.' When I fell on my butt during cheerleading practice, my dad said to me in the car, 'I wonder if it's because you're fat for an Asian.'"[18]

Another influence on body image revolves around expectations of physical shape and attractiveness relating to age. Body image often changes, especially as people get older. Adolescents, for instance, frequently experience growth spurts and body development during teenage years; older adults may develop wrinkles or lose hair. When someone likes a particular thing about his or her body, and then that thing changes, he or she may turn to extreme methods of reversing the change. For example, a 40-year-old man who is starting to get a lot of wrinkles might get Botox to smooth out his skin. This is considered an extreme method because Botox is actually a neurotoxin, or poison, that temporarily paralyzes the face, which causes wrinkles to relax and smooth out.

The Importance of Biology

While customs, fashion, and culture will influence ideas about body images, these influences also must work within other boundaries that affect both body style and the development of body image. For instance, there are far fewer clothing options available to overweight people. Stores such as Target, Wal-Mart, and Kohls sell plus-size clothing, but the clothes do not go much higher than size 3X, and the selection is limited. Some stores, such as Torrid or Lane Bryant, sell fashionable clothes exclusively for larger figures, but they are more expensive. This creates a perception that being fat is wrong, which can contribute to a poor self-image for people whose biology makes them overweight.

It can be difficult for people to find fashionable plus-size clothing in many stores.

Biology is a constant influence on body type. Every person's body type and personal qualities—hair and eye color, shape, and height—are influenced by the genetics and biology of his or her parents. Parents and distant relatives provide the genes that shape and limit the possibilities of one's physical appearance. Some physical traits, such as hair or eye color, are easy to change; hair dye and colored contacts are found in many stores. Other traits, such as height or breast size, are more difficult and require surgery to change permanently. Genes have also been found to influence whether someone is likely to develop an eating disorder.

Besides impacting how bodies grow, Smolak has noted that the strongest connection between biology and body image issues may be indirect. In relation to body image, personality—also called temperament—and biology are also connected. Temperament relates to qualities such as emotion and mood; some people are naturally happier than others and may have an easier time forming a positive body image. This plays into what researchers call the "nature vs. nurture" argument: whether our emotions and behavior are influenced more by biology (nature) or our social environment (nurture). Both play a big role, but no one is sure yet whether one is more important than the other.

The Role of Family and Friends

After biology, one of the earliest influences relating to the formation of body image is a child's family or home environment. Important influences include comments by adults on a child's appearance, modeling (how the parent relates to his or her own body image), and the feedback the child receives from parents and guardians. Johnston has explained, "As individuals ... we each have a unique beauty history. Some of our families were more concerned about looks than others. Growing up, we each received different feedback about our looks from friends and family members."[19] People who receive positive feedback are more likely to have a positive body image.

Peers, including friends and classmates, can also play an important role in the development of body image. As with parents,

Friends who provide emotional support are an important part of creating a positive self-image.

peer feedback and teasing can help shape attitudes and influence body image ideals.

Words Can Either Help or Hurt

One important aspect of parent-child communication in relation to body image is referred to by psychologists as "direct comments." This means that a parent has offered feedback to the child about his or her weight, hair, or general appearance. "Parents can influence body image development by selecting and commenting on children's clothing and appearance, or by requiring the child to look certain ways and to eat or avoid certain foods,"[20] Smolak explained. Some research has suggested that positive comments by parents on a child's weight or appearance can lead to a more positive body image.

However, research has also found that parents or guardians frequently offer negative comments regarding weight, suggesting, for example, that a child should eat less or exercise more in an effort to slim down. These comments may be connected to negative feelings in relation to a child's body image. One study found that

> *teens whose parents talked to them about food with a focus on their weight or size (e.g., "Don't eat that—you'll get fat!" or "Yikes, that's super fattening.") were more likely to fall into body hate, extreme*

Young adults whose parents are critical of their children's bodies are more likely to develop a poor body image.

dieting, and eating disorders. People whose parents didn't talk about size or weight, but just focused on healthfulness of foods, were less likely to have any body-image or eating problems.[21]

Researchers have also wondered whether these direct comments affect boys and girls equally. Some theorists have suggested that women receive more pressure to conform to what is considered an attractive body style within a given culture and because of this, parents may focus their body image comments more directly on girls than boys. A number of studies, however, have shown that parents are equally critical of boys and girls in regard to weight, and according to NEDA, "studies have shown

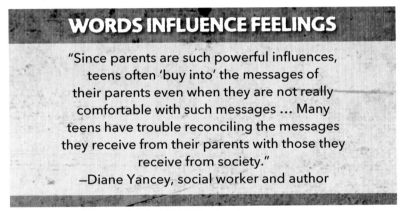

WORDS INFLUENCE FEELINGS

"Since parents are such powerful influences, teens often 'buy into' the messages of their parents even when they are not really comfortable with such messages ... Many teens have trouble reconciling the messages they receive from their parents with those they receive from society."
—Diane Yancey, social worker and author

Diane Yancey, *Eating Disorders*. Brookfield, CT: Twenty-First Century, 1999, p. 69.

an increase in the numbers, although it is uncertain whether more males actually have eating disorders [ED] now or are becoming more aware of the gender-neutral nature of ED."[22]

Direct comments can also come from friends and schoolmates. This feedback can be either positive ("Cool shoes!" or "I really like that dress!") or negative ("Those leggings are ugly," or "You're too fat to be wearing that shirt."). Positive and negative feedback by peers, like direct comments by adults, help shape body image. It is important for friends to support each other by making positive comments about each other's appearance. Body image can have a lifelong impact on self-image. Although Tami L., a library clerk from Buffalo, New York, is an adult, she still remembers how much her classmates' negative comments hurt:

When I was in eighth grade, my female classmates and I were all in the bathroom. We were talking about weight and somebody told me I wasn't "fat-fat." It messed me up. I literally was starving myself. My mom ... explained to me what anorexia was. I didn't want to die. I started eating [again]. Even now, though, the words "not fat-fat" go through my mind. I'm not a thin girl by any means. I worry about my weight and I really think even now it would be so easy to fall into the pattern of the 13-year-old me.[23]

Helpful Advice vs. Body Shaming

It is important to recognize the difference between helpful advice and body shaming. Body shaming involves making someone feel bad about the way he or she looks. Advice about someone's appearance should not be given if someone has not asked for it by saying things such as, "Does this outfit look okay?" or "What kind of haircut should I get?" Examples of helpful advice include: "If you're getting a haircut, I thought your hair looked especially good when it was shoulder length," or "I really like the blue dress best on you." Examples of body shaming include, "You shouldn't eat so much. It's not healthy," and "You'd be a lot prettier if you weren't so bony."

A good rule to remember is that comments should only be made about a person's appearance if it is something you would want someone to say to you. For example, it is acceptable to tell people that they have something stuck in their teeth. It is not acceptable to tell people to change things they cannot immediately change, such as the way they talk or their weight.

Indirect Ways of Influencing Body Image

People do not always learn about body image because of what people say to them out loud. Some methods are much more subtle. Whereas the influence of direct comments by parents and friends may appear fairly straightforward, other influences on the development of body image, such as modeling, are more difficult to measure. Modeling is when a child learns by watching what a parent does or by listening to what a parent says about his or her own body image. By observing a parent's behavior, a child may develop the same habits. If a parent comments frequently on his or her own weight, a child may learn that body weight is something that should be monitored closely. Modeling is also complicated by the fact that a parent may send contradictory messages. For example, a father may say one thing—"Your personality is more important than your looks"—but then offer critical comments about his own weight.

Perhaps the most potentially harmful feedback to one's concept of body image is teasing, whether from family or peers. It has a large impact on adolescents, who may internalize teasing as self-criticism. "Researchers have found that being teased is one of the most commonly reported precipitants of body dissatisfaction,"[24] scientists Stacey Tantleff-Dunn and Jessica L. Gokee have written.

Another issue that impacts the development of body image in both adults and children is peer pressure. Studies have shown peer pressure among teenagers to be influential in the development of behavior such as drinking alcohol, smoking cigarettes, and taking drugs. Many researchers believe that peer pressure may also influence the desire of teenagers to conform to popular body image types. For instance, if one person in a friend group is overweight while all her friends are slender, she may feel like an outsider and want to lose weight to fit in.

Gender and Body Image

When focusing on body image and how body image develops, many researchers have studied whether these issues impact boys and girls differently. In the past, social critics commonly argued that girls and women are taught by their culture to focus on body image more intensely than boys and men. Recently, though, evidence has emerged that just as much pressure is put on boys as on girls. The difference is where women are expected to be very thin, men are expected to be very muscular. Boys who are underweight or naturally thin may feel they are not "manly" enough and turn to dangerous habits, such as abusing steroids or pushing themselves to exercise too much. Additionally, girls struggle more with whether their faces look beautiful than boys do. Thousands of makeup products are marketed to girls, encouraging them to cover up their flaws with foundation and powder. In contrast, while men can wear makeup as well if they choose, it is not widely marketed to them. Many men do not wear it for fear of being labeled "girly," or simply because they do not care enough about it to use it. The emphasis for men is more on their physical and mental abilities, and the beauty standards that are aimed at them focus more on having a muscular body than a flawless face.

Beauty Standards for Girls

Girls are bombarded every day with negative messages about their bodies. Society tells them they need to have slender figures, flawless skin, and perfect hair so they can be desirable to boys. Appearance is often emphasized for girls over intelligence, which can lead to low self-esteem and a belief that they are naturally less smart or less worthy than boys. Society promotes the message that women must be beautiful to be loved, and if they hear it enough, they internalize this message to the extent that one study found that telling straight women that men prefer larger women improved the women's self-image. However, "telling women that other women find larger models attractive does not yield similar benefits,"[25] suggesting that women who are attracted to men care less about whether other women think they are pretty and more about whether men do.

To help fight these messages, Dove soap created an ad campaign called the "Campaign for Real Beauty," featuring models of all shapes, sizes, and colors, as well as several videos about real women. In one, women are separated from a sketch artist by a curtain and he draws them first from their descriptions of themselves, then from someone else's description of them. When the two pictures are placed side by side, it is clear that the women see themselves as less beautiful than other people see them. In another video, signs are placed over two doors that are next to each other. One door says "Beautiful," while the

There is no such thing as the "perfect" body; women can be beautiful no matter what they look like. That is the message behind Dove ads, such as the one shown here.

other says "Average." Dove filmed the women deciding which door to walk through based on their view of themselves. Some women encouraged their friends to choose the "Beautiful" door, which shows how important emotional support is in creating a positive self-image.

Body Image and Boys

While the idea is generally accepted that girls and women experience more body image concerns than boys and men, research suggests that this phenomenon may be changing. Fewer studies have been conducted with boys, but the available research suggests that body image concerns begin in preadolescence for boys. Researchers also note that advertising has focused more heavily on boys and men in recent years. However, because body image has historically been considered an issue only for girls, many men do not want to speak up about it because they do not want to sound feminine. The negative images that boys are shown revolve mostly around being masculine. This includes the emphasis on being tall and muscular. CNBC reported that "17 percent of young men aged 16–24 think male models in advertising have made them more self-conscious of their appearance."[26]

To bring awareness to these issues, the website BuzzFeed posted a video featuring the Try Guys, where four men were Photoshopped according to their ideal body images. Before the photo shoot, they discussed what they considered the ideal male body type to be: athletic, strong, muscular, and not too chubby but not too skinny. After seeing the photos that made them look like this, however, they had mixed emotions and realized that society's ideal body type is just as unrealistic for men as

Getting a very muscular body requires more time and effort than most people are able to commit to.

for women. Keith Habersberger said, "I don't know if I really want to look like that. Maybe I like my soft body more than I thought." Ned Fulmer said, "If I wanted to look like this and have my job and spend time with my family—there's just not enough hours in the day."[27]

Different Standards for Men and Women

Even though society places pressure on both men and women to be youthful and attractive, the standards are different for each sex. Women's appearance is emphasized more than their personality; girls are more likely to be complimented for being pretty than for being smart, and a pretty girl may be seen as less strong and competent. For men, although appearance is seen to be important, more emphasis is placed on their intelligence and ability to do things such as fix cars or take care of their families financially. This goes along with the overall perception that men must appear to be "masculine."

As adults grow older, gender issues may continue to separate the sexes in regard to body image ideals. "Signs of aging in men may be seen to make them look more 'distinguished,'" noted Grogan, "whereas in women (who are often judged in terms of physical attractiveness rather than in terms of abilities or experience), signs of aging may be seen negatively both by others and by themselves."[28] This difference seems to be based on the idea that men are perceived as gaining career-related experience and competency along with a secure economic status as they grow older. In some studies, however, women have been shown to depend less on appearance for self-esteem after 60, perhaps because physical appearance has become less important.

Beauty Standards in the LGBT Community

Lesbian, gay, bisexual, and transgender people have different beauty standards within their community. Lesbians generally fall into two main categories: femme, which means they wear long hair, dresses, and makeup; and butch, which means they wear short hair and clothes that are masculine or androgynous. There is a stereotype in the media that lesbian couples always involve one butch and one femme partner, but this is not true; two butch girls or two femme girls can and often do date. A. Kelly, a member of the LGBT community, noted that "lesbians can and do often follow the very same beauty standards that straight women do, though studies have shown lesbians feel less pressure in regards to body image and are far less likely to see themselves as overweight/have less internalized social ideas of attractiveness compared to [straight women]."[29] Bisexual or pansexual girls face the same standards as lesbians, but bisexuals tend to fall more on the femme side.

Lesbians often dress either butch or femme, but there does not have to be one of each in a relationship.

Gay men, like straight men, are expected to be muscular, but this pressure is often much stronger for gay men. Our culture currently frowns on men who look and act very feminine, and this standard is true even in the LGBT community. Gay men often feel that they should be very attractive and muscular, which can lead them to develop eating disorders or abuse steroids.

Standards for transgender people are similar to those for cisgender, or non-trans, people, but the pressure is much higher, as it is for gay men. According to Kelly, "where cis women can skip painting their nails or wearing makeup, trans women who miss painting their nails or wear jeans for a therapy session can risk losing their hormone treatments for months or years if their therapist believes this to be proof they are 'lying' about their gender." This type of pressure can also come from friends and family; a trans teen girl who does not always wear skirts may be told that she is clearly confused or lying, even though no one says the same about cis girls who wear jeans. Genderfluid people may get the same type of comments, since they alternate between dressing as girls and as boys. Additionally, "trans men ... are often read as butch lesbians and have their gender ignored," Kelly said, which can lead to insecurity about their bodies. She also noted:

> While there is now more representation for trans people in the media and in the public conscience, its very focused on a Eurocentric [focusing on Europe] view of beauty, with thin, white, stereotypically attractive people who pass as cisgender given much more visibility and acceptance than trans people who don't fit into those groups. There is also a heavy focus on people passing in very specific ways, and people who do not fit those standards face many more challenges than people who easily can.[30]

Health Affects Body Image

With all of the negativity surrounding bodies, it can be difficult to form a positive self-image. This is why positive direct comments from friends and family are so important. A strong emotional support network goes a long way toward reinforcing body positivity. There is nothing wrong with people loving themselves as they are, just like there is nothing wrong with them deciding that they want to make a change to their appearance. Health is more important than body type, and weight is not always an accurate indication of health. Ashley W., a mother from Buffalo,

All Body Types Encounter Shaming

Fat shaming has a long history in our culture, especially on the Internet. People post photos and comments telling overweight people that they are not as good as thin people and may even say such hurtful things to people's faces. It is common for some people to follow up these comments by saying, "I'm just concerned about your health." Others may post photos of their flat stomachs online with the phrase, "What's your excuse?"

Thin people experience body shaming as well. Phrases such as "Real women have curves" have arisen in response to fat shaming, claiming that women who are seen as too skinny are not good enough for men. Even very fit people—both men and women—are sometimes shamed for being too muscular by people who think it is not "normal" to have visible muscles or that fit people are trying too hard to change themselves when they were "already skinny enough."

In reality, there is no such thing as a perfect body type. There is also no such thing as a body type that is universally attractive to either men or women. Someone's weight or body type is not a true measure of his or her worth as a person or of how healthy he or she is.

New York, recalled the negative comments she received before she gained weight:

When I was younger and [thinner], I used to force myself to eat because I was tired of being told how "I'd never understand weight problems" and I looked too thin ... I've always struggled the most with my confidence when I was thin because that's when people felt it was ok to comment ... People used to tell me, "You're way too skinny, why don't you go and eat something?" or "Eat a cheeseburger." It was annoying and insulting and made me self-conscious, and in reality I was much healthier when I was slim than I am now.[31]

However, it is important to remember that even if someone is unhealthy, he or she is not a bad person. Some people may be underweight and unhealthy, but they have trouble gaining weight because of their genetics. Others may be overweight due to a thyroid condition, which makes it difficult for them to lose weight, or because they have binge eating disorder, which makes it hard for them to stop eating. Still others have diseases that make them unhealthy in other ways; for example, a person with fibromyalgia may be too tired to do many physical activities.

It is impossible to know exactly what another person is struggling with unless they tell people, but they do not owe that explanation to anyone. People often accuse others of being lazy or not wanting to be healthy, then find out that someone struggles with a disorder and say, "I didn't know the challenges you were facing! If I had known, I wouldn't have said those things." It is important for people to assume from the start that they do not know all the challenges someone is dealing with so they do not body shame someone for something they cannot control. Because a healthy body is the "ideal" body in our culture, someone who is unhealthy for any reason may already have a very negative self-image.

The Role of Media in Shaping Body Image

Just as modeling takes place within the family, it can also take place through the media. The overwhelming majority of movie and TV stars are thin, and the ones who are not may often be the butt of jokes onscreen. However, "fat" is also sometimes used as a weapon in movies, shows, and magazines against people who have an average body weight. For example, comedienne Amy Schumer is frequently referred to as plus-size or fat when she actually has an average body type. Comments such as these may cause insecurity in people who are the same size as those celebrities.

Even when characters are not explicitly being called fat, it is clear there are still certain standards in media for body type. Comic books and video games, especially ones featuring superheroes, are notorious for overemphasizing women's bodies and drawing female characters in outfits that are impractical for fighting crime, while the focus for male characters is their ability to fight. One website, The Hawkeye Initiative, is attempting to draw attention to this double standard by drawing male characters in the same style as female characters, showing how ridiculous the poses and outfits are.

For men, the focus is almost entirely on a muscular body. Characters without much muscle definition are often teased onscreen for being weak or feminine. For example, in *Captain America: The First Avenger*, Steve Rogers is too weak for the army and is portrayed as not being attractive to women before he receives the super soldier serum. Thin, less muscular males may sometimes be placed together with female characters who are very muscular, teasing both the man for being too weak and the woman for being too masculine. Cartoons also sometimes

Captain America: The First Avenger *shows Steve Rogers as being more popular and attractive after he becomes taller and more muscular.*

show women leaving their skinny boyfriends for more muscular men. All of these messages can have a strong impact on viewers' self-image.

The media also has a large role in how people see other factors related to body image, such as race, religion, and sexual orientation. By focusing more on people of one particular type than another—for instance, there are very few Native Americans in Hollywood—the media shapes how people view themselves and others.

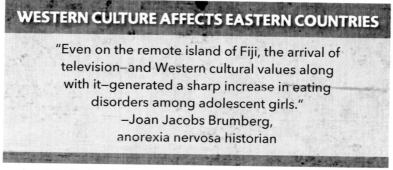

WESTERN CULTURE AFFECTS EASTERN COUNTRIES

"Even on the remote island of Fiji, the arrival of television–and Western cultural values along with it–generated a sharp increase in eating disorders among adolescent girls."
–Joan Jacobs Brumberg,
anorexia nervosa historian

Joan Jacobs Brumberg, *Fasting Girls: The History of Anorexia Nervosa*, rev. ed. New York, NY: Vintage, 2000, p. xv.

How Important Is the Media?

In 2015, CNN reported that in a study of kids ages 8 to 18 in the United States, those surveyed spent about nine hours per day using media. This can include the Internet, TV, movies, books, magazines, music, and video games. Many people assert that the media is the leading cause of negative body image and low self-esteem, especially for women. Other social critics see the media as an easy scapegoat for broader social problems. Author Brian Cuban wrote about his own struggle with body image in the 1970s, before televisions and the Internet were in every home:

What was the environmental influence in this warped reflection of [myself]? It was the fat shaming by my mother when I was a child at home. It was the weight bullying, including physical assault, by other kids at school. It was the desire to be accepted by the kids I saw every day: the popular kids, the kids who went to prom, the kids walking down the school hallway holding hands. I wanted that, I didn't feel worthy of it, and I went to dire lengths in an effort to convince others (and myself) that I had value.[32]

Ways to Respond to Shaming

At one point or another, everyone will face comments from friends, family, and even strangers about some part of his or her appearance. People whose appearance does not match up with the cultural ideal will face this more often. Here are some responses to comments such as, "You would be prettier if you wore makeup," "Why don't you ever straighten your hair?" or "How much do you weigh?"

- "That's a personal question, and I don't want to answer it."
- "It's none of your business."
- "Maybe you didn't realize, but comments like that are really hurtful. I'm proud of who I am."
- "Why do you care?"
- "The way I look doesn't have any effect on your life, so please stop talking about it."
- "I didn't ask for your opinion."
- "I'm just not interested in [wearing makeup/ lifting weights/straightening hair/etc.]"
- "I do it because I want to [wear makeup/lift weights/straighten hair/etc.]"

Remember that it is okay to walk away without answering, and getting upset is a normal reaction. To feel better, do things that make you feel good, such as wearing your hair in your favorite style, going out with friends who accept and love you, or treating yourself to a movie.

The rise in popularity of social media in recent years is giving an outlet to people who want to challenge Hollywood's portrayal of beauty. More than ever, people are sharing photos of themselves that challenge the standard beauty ideal seen on TV, in movies, and in advertisements. It seems as though these changes are slowly being picked up by the media; for example, Melissa McCarthy is an incredibly popular plus-size actress, and she has starred in roles that do not revolve around her size. However, body shaming is still a problem, and one part of the solution may be for movies, TV, and magazines to start showing more diversity in body types.

The Media Is Not Reality

Many media observers say that a central problem with the daily bombardment of body images is that the media often fails to represent all body types equally. Kate Fox, writing for the Social Issues Research Centre, noted the perceived influence of the media:

- *Thanks to the media, we have become used to extremely strict and identical standards of beauty.*

- *TV, billboards, magazines etc. mean that we see "beautiful people" all the time, more often than members of our own family, making exceptional good looks seem real, normal and attainable.*

- *Standards of beauty have in fact become harder and harder to attain, particularly for women. The current media ideal of thinness for women is achievable by less than 5 percent of the female population.*[33]

The majority of people in ads look like this, even though the majority of the population doesn't.

Female models in fashion magazines may be mostly white, tall, and thin; men are mostly white and muscular with flat stomachs. Minorities are very underrepresented, even though they make up almost half of the American population. "These images convey assumptions about what is desirable in our physical selves while dispensing with reality,"[34] science writer Brandon Keim noted. Because of makeup and plastic surgery, actors and models may appear to never age or gain weight. The media, these critics say, idealizes body types in order to sell products or increase ratings.

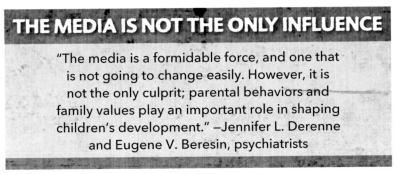

THE MEDIA IS NOT THE ONLY INFLUENCE

"The media is a formidable force, and one that is not going to change easily. However, it is not the only culprit; parental behaviors and family values play an important role in shaping children's development." –Jennifer L. Derenne and Eugene V. Beresin, psychiatrists

Jennifer L. Derenne and Eugene V. Beresin, "Body Image, Media, and Eating Disorders," *Academic Psychiatry*, June 2006. ap.psychiatryonline.org/cgi/content/full/30/3/257.

These critics also believe that continuous exposure to ideal body types in the media may lead men and women to internalize these images. Johnston wrote, "Appearance pressures in our society can easily turn into chronic dissatisfaction with our appearance and a never-ending pursuit of self-improvement."[35]

Achieving the slimness or muscular build of a fashion or fitness model, however, may not be realistic or even healthy for many people, health specialists emphasize. Getting the perfect look, for instance, may be both time consuming and hard work: "Some actors spend as many as three hours in the gym per day to lose weight, and it is all done with a licensed trainer at their side, commenting on their form and suggesting workout options to them."[36] Many models and actors enhance their appearance with cosmetic surgery and liposuction (the removal of fat by cosmetic surgery), have personal trainers, and are able to dedicate several hours each day to working out. Photographs of models and actors in magazines are further altered with Photoshop. It is common knowledge that Photoshop is used on just about every magazine or ad photo, but some actors and actresses deny it because they prefer for people to think that the retouched version is how they look naturally. Jennifer Lawrence is one exception; when she appeared in an ad for Dior, she laughed when she saw the finished product and said, "Of course it's Photoshop; people don't look like that."[37] When men and women compare themselves to media figures and attempt to copy difficult or impossible standards, this can lead to a negative body image and low self esteem.

Jennifer Lawrence has not made a secret of the fact that the ads she appears in are Photoshopped.

Clothes and Body Image

The type of clothes a person wears can impact his or her body image just as much as other parts of his or her appearance. Many people think that having a certain brand name on their clothes will make them cool or popular, and not having those clothes can negatively affect their self-image. When people wear clothes that fit them well, they often look and feel better than when they wear clothes that do not, even if the clothes that do not fit them are fashionable. Religion also plays a role in the way people choose to dress. Many religions emphasize modesty, particularly for women. For Muslims, this may mean wearing a hijab, or headscarf, although not all women choose to do this. For devout Christians, this might mean wearing longer skirts and high-cut shirts. There is nothing wrong with choosing to dress modestly and interpreting "modest" in different ways; for example, a Christian girl may think that a knee-length dress is appropriate, while a Muslim girl may not wear anything shorter than ankle-length. What is important is that these are personal choices that everyone has to make for herself. Sometimes men may tell women that it is their responsibility to cover themselves so men do not get distracted, but this is simply false. Men, like women, are responsible for their own actions, and it is not a woman's responsibility to change her behavior or appearance in order to protect a man from certain thoughts or behaviors.

Groups That Are Underrepresented in the Media

The vast majority of actors, actresses, and models are tall, white, and thin, with perfect facial features and no obvious disabilities. This ignores the majority of the population. For instance, according to the Centers for Disease Control and Prevention, "2.2 million people in the United States depend on a wheelchair for day-to-day tasks and mobility."[38] However, characters in wheelchairs are rare onscreen and in books and magazines, and when they do appear, the focus is usually on their disability rather than their personality. The same is true for deaf people; rarely are they featured in the media unless the plot calls for someone to know sign language. Some actors with Down syndrome have won roles on TV, but they are not often cast.

People of color are also underrepresented. Often they are cast as villains, and sometimes they are erased completely. When Hollywood casts white actors in non-white roles, this is called whitewashing. For example, in the classic movie *Breakfast at Tiffany's*, Mickey Rooney, a white actor, played a Japanese character. Whitewashing is also the term for when a magazine or ad lightens a dark-skinned person's skin and hair so he or she appears to be more white. These practices send a message to non-white viewers and readers that they are not as valued as white people. Many black, Indian, and Asian people use cosmetic skin whiteners to try to make themselves appear lighter because having dark skin gives them a poor self-image.

Muslims are one of the groups that are rarely seen in popular movies and TV shows.

Dwarves are slowly gaining visibility in Hollywood with the success of TV shows such as *Little People, Big World*, but they are still not widely cast unless the role revolves around their height. Peter Dinklage, who is best known for playing Tyrion Lannister on *Game of Thrones*, refused to take any roles for leprechauns or elves because they made a joke out of people of his height. It is still very rare for a little person to be cast in a role that does not explicitly mention their height, or that gives them a love interest, particularly one who is of average height.

LGBT people are also increasingly visible in the media, but only in very specific roles. Transsexual or transgender people are very rarely mentioned, and gay people are usually heavily stereotyped and frequently the butt of jokes. Kelly noted that "the media offers a very narrow idea of beauty standards for gay men … with shows often showing only the stereotypical femme gay man or the very masculine man who appears to be straight turning out to be gay, often as a joke or a way to shock the viewer."[39] Similarly, lesbian women are almost always shown as masculine, or butch.

These are only a few of the groups that are not widely seen in the media. Their absence can have a significant effect on people who identify with them because it implies that they are not important or "normal." Additionally, it affects how people who are not part of those groups see them, leading to offensive stereotypes. When people see these stereotypes modeled onscreen or in books and hear hurtful things that other people say to them based on negative media portrayals, it can be harmful to their body image.

The Gradual Change of Media

Some social observers have been quick to point out that the media has been an easy scapegoat for broader societal problems. A number of sociologists have stated that the ideas relating to body image in the media are simply a reflection of values within the larger culture. That would mean thin models in magazines and muscular men on television are ideals that society has already embraced, and the media simply reinforces these ideals.

This creates a vicious cycle where the media only portrays the impossible standards of beauty held by one generation, which is the only thing the next generation sees in the media, causing them to embrace those roles as well and causing the media to keep showing them.

One key to breaking this cycle is to let movie producers and magazine publishers know that the current beauty ideal is not something society supports anymore. A number of actors have been outspoken critics on the media's portrayal of body images. Actors such as Tina Fey and Mindy Kaling have made a public issue out of the media's focus on thin women. In Fey's memoir *Bossypants*, she described all the work that goes into a photo shoot and how it creates an illusion: "Don't ever feel inadequate when you look at magazines. Just remember that every person you see on a cover has a bra and underwear hanging out a gaping hole in the back."[40] Kaling discussed how upset she felt at a photo shoot where all of the dresses were too small for her: "I went into a [bathroom] stall, sat down on a … toilet, and cried. Why didn't I just lose 20 pounds so I never had to be in this situation again? Life was so much easier for actresses who did that."[41]

As a result of criticism from actors and health officials, and because of general social concern for healthier body images, the media has attempted to change its approach to body image in a number of instances. Several fashion magazines that feature plus-size models have been launched, including *Plus*, *Venus Diva*, and *World of Curves*; the number of fat jokes

As an Indian woman who has an average body type, Kaling has said in interviews that she has been asked about her body image more than about the work she does.

onscreen has declined; and there is more diversity in movies and TV than in past years, although there is still a long way to go. However, it seems that social media is playing an increasingly large role in shaping body image in both negative and positive ways. Seeing harsh comments on photos of people who are average size but perceived to be overweight can have the same negative effect as when average characters on TV are called fat, and it can be difficult to tell whether Facebook or Instagram pictures have been edited to make the person appear naturally more beautiful, which can create unrealistic ideals. However, people who post positive messages and photos have a chance of reaching a wider audience and letting others know that they do not have to live up to the unattainable media standards to be beautiful.

The Media Sends Mixed Messages

While critics have noted that many of these changes in representing body image may be motivated by an attempt to sell products to new consumers, they have nonetheless greeted many of these changes as positive. Overall, these changes have allowed the media to display a wider variety of body styles.

Even with these changes, however, media messages about body image remain conflicted. One common complaint is that fashion and fitness magazines publish articles about focusing on health more than weight or exploring the dangers of steroid use, while still featuring photo spreads of ultra-thin models and overly muscular men. Even in magazines featuring plus-size models, advertisements may send out inconsistent messages. "On one hand the magazine celebrates beauty and fashion at every size," noted an anonymous commenter on the social technology and media website Viewpoints, "but [on] the other hand, [it] is indicating that we cannot possibly be happy to be plus size and that we must be on Weight Watchers."[42] Many plus-size models are also not larger than the average woman, which affects how women see themselves.

These conflicting messages and others like them underline one last problem with understanding the media's influence on body image issues: The media seldom delivers an unchanging body image message. Because of this nonuniform message and the variety of body images presented, some media observers have suggested that people have vastly different experiences with the media and how it affects their body image.

CHAPTER 4

The Problem with Advertising

Although the media and advertising are intertwined, advertising is directly concerned with selling products, while the media is mainly for entertainment. Ads can be found everywhere, including magazines, billboards, buses, benches, on TV, and online. They can also be found within the media; for example, a particular clothing line may provide the wardrobe for a popular TV actress, making people want to buy the type of clothes she wears so they can imitate her look.

Many advertisements use models who live up to the cultural standard of beauty to sell the products. This can make people insecure about their own body, so they buy the product if they think it will change how their body looks. Other times, they buy the product because they are attracted to the person in the ad. However, seeing all of these tall, thin, mostly white models in ads can contribute to a poor body image, since advertisements sometimes rely on making people feel bad about their body. This is also a dangerous industry for the models, who are constantly told they need to be thinner. People who are viewing these ads and wishing for the model's body may not realize that in some cases, the model has been starving herself.

Some progress has been made recently on changing this culture. The *New York Times* reported that a Gucci ad was banned in Britain because "the Advertising Standards Authority ... ruled that the ad was 'irresponsible' and that the model looked 'unhealthily thin,' fanning a perennial debate in the fashion industry over when thin is too thin."[43] France has also put regulations in place, requiring models to provide a doctor's note saying they are healthy enough to work and banning agencies from hiring anyone who does not have one. France also requires Photoshopped pictures to be labeled.

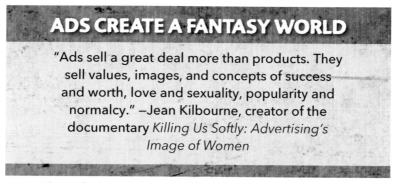

ADS CREATE A FANTASY WORLD

"Ads sell a great deal more than products. They sell values, images, and concepts of success and worth, love and sexuality, popularity and normalcy." —Jean Kilbourne, creator of the documentary *Killing Us Softly: Advertising's Image of Women*

Jean Kilbourne, "Beauty … and the Beast of Advertising," Center for Media Literacy. www.medialit.org/reading-room/beautyand-beast-advertising.

In many countries, the public has often criticized the use of sex or sexuality in advertising, complaining that these images objectify male and female bodies and sexualize adolescent bodies. Furthermore, since advertisers frequently use thin female models and muscular male models, these advertisements set up unrealistic goals and help create body image dissatisfaction. The vast majority of advertising is also heteronormative, meaning that it idealizes traditional gender roles and beauty standards—where people want men to look and act one way and women to look and act a different way—and ignores the LGBT community. Most advertising is designed to get women to buy a product so they can attract a man, or vice versa. Women in advertising are almost always feminine, with long hair, makeup, and dresses, even though some lesbians are butch. Butch lesbians may receive the message, either from advertisements or direct comments from friends and relatives, that they are ugly because they dress like men, and femme lesbians may meet people who believe that all lesbians are butch, therefore femme lesbians cannot be real lesbians.

Because gay men feel the same pressure as straight men to be strong and fit, only more intensely, they are not immune to the ads that show muscular men as the ideal body type, and because of this, many may develop eating disorders or turn to steroids.

The Beginning of Miss America

In 1921 in Atlantic City, New Jersey, a group of community leaders decided on a scheme to promote tourism over Labor Day weekend. The idea was a beauty contest, originally called the Atlantic City Pageant, but later renamed Miss America. Although the idea for a beauty pageant was not new, the evolution of the Miss America pageant modernized the idea of a beauty contest by initiating swimsuit and other competitions. The pageant was first televised in 1955, and during the 1960s, it was one of the highest rated programs on television. Despite the growing popularity of the program, however, social critics wondered whether the Miss America contest truly represented all American women.

The contest rules for Miss America had frequently placed a number of limitations on contestants, including age, height, and weight. For much of the contest's history, limitations were also placed on skin color, and the issue of ethnicity was suppressed. Early Miss America contestants, then, were overwhelmingly white, Anglo-Saxon, and Protestant, a combination commonly referred to as WASP. For this reason, the Miss America contest has often been accused of offering a narrow idea of body image in the United States.

Advertising Targets Young Adults

Author Alissa Quart has written, "The marketing of products to teenagers has existed since the word teenager was coined by Madison Avenue in 1941."[44] Magazines such as *Girls' Life*, *Seventeen*, *Cosmo Girl*, *Teen Vogue*, *Sports Illustrated Kids*, *MH-18*, and *Boys' Life* imitate adult magazines with similar names, but target their ads at young adults. Like advertisements for adults, advertisements for teens and preteens in magazines, radio, and television use body images in an attempt to sell everything from soft drinks to makeup to MP3 players.

Relying on body image in advertising for the teen market has perhaps been even more controversial than advertising for adults. Many social critics believe that advertisers play on teens'

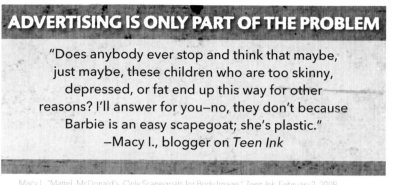

insecurities to sell products that promise to make the young consumer more attractive. Furthermore, they argue, advertising to young adults bypasses parental oversight. Others argue that teens are capable of understanding the methods advertisers use and that buying products to enhance body image builds self-esteem.

Vanity Sizing

One trend in the fashion world that has caused a lot of negative body issues is the fact that women's clothing sizes are different from brand to brand. Men's clothing is sized by the measurements of the person's body, but women's sizes are just numbers or letters such as 12, 14, S, XS, etc. Because these do not really mean anything, different brands can use different measurements and put the same size on it. For example, a person may wear size 12 jeans from Target, but size 8 jeans from Old Navy. This is sometimes known as vanity sizing because people believe that the stores are trying to make people feel better about wearing bigger sizes; however, manufacturers say it is just because different companies have a different range of sizes. Whether or not the clothes are marked smaller on purpose, the different sizes can negatively affect a person's body image and make it discouraging and time-consuming to find clothes that fit correctly.

The Modeling Industry

One common method of using body image to help sell commercial products to children and adults is the use of models in fashion magazines. Fashion magazines such as *Glamour* and *Elle* feature multiple layouts of models wearing new lines of clothing. Male models appear in the same fashion magazines as women, while also appearing in the advertisements of men's magazines such as *GQ*.

As with media criticism, a number of arguments have begun around the issue of whether models affect men's and women's concepts of body image. Some social critics and psychologists believe these models set an unhealthy example. Michelle Lee, a former *Glamour* and *Mademoiselle* editor, has stated, "A woman between the ages of 18 and 34 has a 1 percent chance of being as thin as a super model. Nearly 50 percent of all teenage girls in one study said they wanted to lose weight after viewing magazines, when only 29 percent were overweight."[45] ABC News notes that the average model weighs 23 percent less than the average woman, compared to 8 percent 20 years ago. Plus-size models are between sizes 6 and 14, which do not reflect actual

Models and actresses have a team of people whose only job is to make them look beautiful.

plus sizes. Since clothing stores base the sizes they carry on the fashion industry, it can be very difficult for average or plus-size women to find clothing that fits them.

While models and actors can be intimidating to someone who feels he or she will never measure up to that standard, it is important to remember that looking pretty and fashionable is a full-time job for them. The perfect look requires a great deal of effort, and models expend a great deal of time to achieve it. "Every model must spend hours each day on personal care," writer Ian Halperin has noted. "Cosmetics, skin care, hair care, body care, and fragrances are a daily routine."[46] After understanding these requirements, critics argue most people do not expect to look like a model. Eugene Lee Yang from the Try Guys noted, "I am of the opinion that these things are attainable if you have the time and the money and the team to constantly work out and get ... abs. It's just that no one's that rich or has that much time except for celebrities and actors and models. It's not our job to look that good ... People aren't just going to remember you because you have six-pack abs. They remember you because you're a good person."[47]

Furthermore, models and images of models may be enhanced in a number of ways. Many enhance appearances with cosmetic surgery and liposuction. Photographs of models in American magazines are always Photoshopped unless otherwise noted, sometimes in ways that are extremely noticeable. In another BuzzFeed video, the Try Guys recreated some pictures where the models had been retouched to try to give them a more idealized look. The makeup artists and photographers were purposely hard on them to mimic what a model has to go through. During the photo shoot, Ned said, "I just felt so beaten down and like there were expectations of me that I couldn't meet." Eugene remarked, "Everything you think is real is constructed." After seeing the retouched photos, Zach Kornfeld said, "If one of these women were to release a photo of just what she looked like when she rolled out of bed, it would be considered brave, as opposed to just human." Keith Habersberger shared his takeaway from the project: "You can't judge your raw self with someone else's affected self."[48]

Skin, Hair, and Body Image

Besides having impossibly thin bodies, male and female models have flawless skin. Much of this is achieved with the help of makeup artists, who cover up any freckles or blemishes. However, some of it is also done through Photoshop, where wrinkles and acne are removed and skin is given a "glow" so the model appears healthier. There are hundreds of acne products marketed specifically to young adults that promise clearer skin and make a point of talking about how unattractive acne is, which can have a negative impact on how people with acne view themselves. This can lead people to believe that they must wear makeup at all times in order to be pretty. There are many girls and some boys who enjoy wearing makeup and feel that it can be an artistic way to express themselves, and there is nothing wrong with this. It is only a problem when someone feels that his or her face is not good enough to be seen without makeup. The mixed messages that women sometimes receive from men about makeup can contribute to these feelings of not measuring

This woman's face has been made smoother and the eyebrow on the right side of the picture has been shaped in Photoshop.

up. Some men will say that they prefer women who look natural and that makeup is "false advertising." However, these men do not often realize that the women they see in ads who appear to have a natural look are actually wearing makeup. When they say they want a "natural" look, often they mean that they want someone who is naturally flawless, and no one is. Additionally, the claim that makeup is false advertising implies people are products, and this is simply untrue. Women who like to wear makeup are not advertising themselves to people they want to date; they are doing something that makes them feel confident and happy.

Models in ads are also always free of extra body hair. Women are encouraged to shave or wax their legs, their armpits, and under their nose or chin; shape their eyebrows by tweezing or waxing; and keep their bikini line trimmed. The pressure to do this is so strong, especially regarding leg and armpit shaving, that it stops being a choice for most people. Preteen girls are often taught how to shave by their mothers or friends and are told that they are expected to keep doing it for the rest of their lives. Some may do it less often in winter, but if they plan to show their legs at all, they will usually make it a point to shave them. Since so many people do this, it is often not noticeable how strong of a taboo hairy legs are until someone stops shaving and starts receiving criticism from friends, family, and even strangers. This standard is confusing, since arm hair is usually not considered as bad as leg hair, even though it is exactly the same thing.

The fact that models tend to be white can also contribute to a poor body image for people of color. The fashion industry sets the standards for many products. Because so many models are white, underwear or makeup that is beige is often labeled "nude" or "skin-tone," even though it does not reflect everyone's skin color. Both male and female models also tend to have smooth, shiny hair. As with leg and armpit shaving, it is hard to notice how much emphasis is put on hair and the double standards for men and women until someone fails to live up to the "ideal" body image. Girls who get cancer and lose their hair may feel very insecure about themselves and wear wigs or scarves because society tells them it is fine for a man to be bald, but not for a woman. Any woman who shaves her head by choice will probably receive negative comments and may even be mistaken for someone with cancer because it is difficult for people to understand why she would choose to get rid of her hair. Thin hair is also a source of poor body image for both men and women because so many models have or appear to have very thick hair.

Many average white men and women have trouble getting their hair to look the same as a model's, but for black women, the problem goes deeper. Many black women are given the impression, both from the media and from direct comments, that their natural hair is not pretty and they should relax or straighten it. This can be very stressful and time-consuming; one blogger wrote, "Taking care of my natural hair has made me so obsessed [that] I often struggle with balancing my hair regimen with life's demands like sleep, spending time with my loved ones, personal time, and work."[49] As with makeup, there is no problem with someone wanting to relax her hair, but the feeling that her natural self is ugly and she is required to change her hair creates a negative body image. One study found that "because black women, especially dark-skinned black women, deviate furthest from European beauty standards [of white skin and straight

Nonprofit organizations such as Black Girls Rock!, Black Girls CODE, and At the Well were created to help black girls and women connect and support each other.

hair], they are more likely to experience self-hate, distorted body image, depression, and eating disorders."[50] Organizations such as Black Girls Rock! have been created to help fight these problems.

Advertising Creates a Narrow Range of Beauty

The models that people see in ads do not represent a large portion of our society, but they have set the standard for what we believe people "should" look like. Most of these standards were created only to sell products—for example, women shave their legs because of aggressive marketing campaigns in the 1940s and 1950s designed to sell razors to women by telling them their leg hair was ugly. Advertising is a powerful tool that can change the way people see the world.

Even if ads themselves do not directly influence how a person sees himself or herself, they shape the way our culture sees beauty. Many people do not care whether or not they look like celebrities, but they do care about whether the people they interact with on a daily basis find them attractive. A woman with hairy legs, a dark-skinned black woman, an underweight boy, or a person of average weight who is considered to be fat may all receive criticism from friends, family, and strangers in person or on the Internet. These types of comments have a strong impact on a person's self-image.

However, it seems as though social media is slowly changing the face of advertising. According to *Fashion* magazine, Caitlyn Jenner and transgender model Andreja Pejic were both asked to be spokeswomen for makeup companies, and more plus-size models who are actually larger than the average woman are being featured in magazines such as *Sports Illustrated* and *People*. Madeline Stuart, an Australian girl with Down syndrome, was offered numerous modeling contracts after the *Australia Daily Mail* published a story about her wish to be a model. Blogs have appeared that remind girls their looks are not the most important thing about them and they have the right to make their own choices about which trends they want to follow. A British ad campaign called "This Girl Can" shows women of all sizes exercising in ways that do not emphasize looking good while working out. It is important to remember that personal preference in appearance is more important than what other people might think.

Madeline Stuart became one of the first models with Down syndrome.

Consequences of Poor Body Image

It is normal for people to want to look their best, and the definition of "best" varies from person to person. The body positive movement is trying to widen the range of body types that Western society finds beautiful, but it has a long way to go; there are still certain characteristics that are seen as "better" than others. "It's a fact that physical attractiveness is prized in our culture," Johnston wrote. "There is nothing wrong with wanting to 'look good.'"[51] In contemporary culture, however, a number of social critics such as Johnston believe that concern over appearance has become an obsession. This has the potential to lead to a number of problems connected to body image issues.

Low self-esteem is the major factor that contributes to body disorders. People who do not receive much positive reinforcement from friends and family often have lower self-esteem. Research has found that "people with low self-esteem are more troubled by failure and tend to exaggerate events as being negative. For example, they often interpret non-critical comments as critical."[52] This means that someone may see certain comments as body shaming when they are not intended to be, which can lower self-esteem more, creating a vicious cycle. People with low self-esteem may feel that they need to take extreme measures in order to change their appearance, including cosmetic surgery, crash diets, or steroid abuse. Other types of disorders, such as binge eating disorder, are a way for people to deal with the shame they feel about their bodies when they believe that there is nothing they can do to change themselves.

America's Obesity Problem

In recent years, doctors have drawn attention to a growing population—both in the United States and around the world—of obese adults. Many have referred to this change as an "obesity epidemic." Generally speaking, anyone with a body mass index (BMI) of 25 or more is considered overweight; anyone with a BMI of 30 or more is considered obese. According to the World Health Organization, over 1 billion adults in the world are overweight, 600 million of whom qualify as obese.

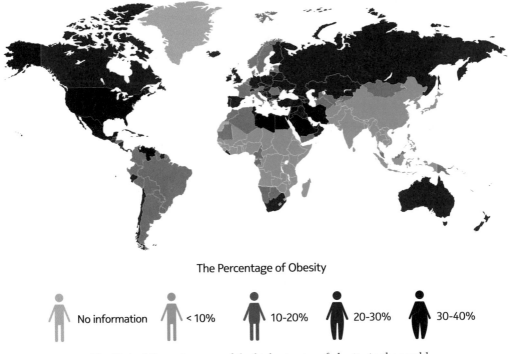

The Percentage of Obesity

No information   < 10%   10-20%   20-30%   30-40%

The United States has one of the highest rates of obesity in the world.

Several reasons have been given for the rise in obesity. For many people around the world, access to food, including foods rich in fats and sugars, is more readily available than at any other time in human history. Portions in restaurants are up to three times larger than they were 20 years ago, which makes people think that a normal portion size is larger than it actually is. The availability of food is further complicated by less physically active lifestyles. As opposed to working all day on a farm as many Americans did during the 1800s, many work in an office behind a desk. Most students sit at their desks for the majority of the day and take buses or cars to and from school, rather than walking or riding their bikes. People who do not like sports will generally turn to sedentary, or less active, entertainment, such as reading and video games, and will often snack on unhealthy foods while doing so. Sedentary activities are not bad, but if students do not do any physical activity outside of gym class, they may find that they are gaining weight.

The obesity epidemic has also had an important impact on body image. Because of this epidemic and because of the health-related problems associated with it, including heart trouble and diabetes, the increase in obesity has also focused greater attention on bodies and, as a result, more attention on body image.

The Dangers of Dieting

Dieting is one thing that many people do to lose weight. It is difficult to get accurate statistics on dieters, but "the Boston Medical Center indicates that [about] 45 million Americans diet each year and spend $33 billion on weight-loss products."[53] Dieting is often seen as a good thing because people believe it shows self-control and a desire to be healthy. In reality, many diets are unhealthy because people do not research them properly. All food and drink consumed in a day make up a person's diet, but when people talk about being "on a diet," they typically mean that they are changing their eating habits for a short period of time in order to lose weight. This means that either they have to stick to that diet for good in order to maintain their weight loss, or they gain the weight back when they return to their old habits.

For some people, a diet may consist of no more than limiting fatty foods and desserts. Others may limit proteins or carbohydrates or substitute a diet product such as Slim-Fast for one or more meals. In extreme cases, dieters reduce calorie intake to 1,000 calories or less per day. These are called "crash diets" or "yo-yo diets," and they can be very dangerous, especially when the dieter is not taking in enough nutrients to support the level of exercise he or she is doing. This type of diet and exercise combination can put stress on the cardiovascular and immune systems. Other types of diets are known as detoxes or cleanses, which falsely promise to boost the body's metabolism and get rid of toxic material that gets left behind in the body. The truth is that the body is able to get rid of toxins without any outside help. Detoxes do not do anything helpful; they are only a way for companies to make money by playing on people's insecurities about their bodies.

Because dieting has become both popular and common, diet aids, books, and supplements have grown into a multibillion-dollar industry. These are often known as "fad diets" because they are very popular for a relatively short period of time, until people realize that they are too difficult to keep up with or are not working at all. They promise to help people lose weight quickly, sometimes up to 10 pounds (4.5 kg) per week. This is very unhealthy and experts recommend losing no more than 2 pounds (0.9 kg) per week, although a person who is overweight may lose more when he or she first starts a healthy diet and exercise routine. Many fad diets rely on severely limiting calories—making people lose a lot of weight quickly because they are starving themselves—or drinking a lot of water, so people lose water weight, which they quickly gain back when they eat. These diets are not recommended by doctors because they generally do not have scientific research to back them up and are unhealthy. Most of them cut out one or more of the food groups, so they are not balanced. Some of the more extreme examples include:

- the raw food diet—only uncooked foods are allowed, limiting food choices mostly to raw fruits, vegetables, and nuts

- the blood type diet—foods are limited based on blood type (For instance, people with type O blood cannot eat wheat, and people with type B blood cannot eat corn or chicken.)

- the lunar diet—changing eating habits based on the phases of the moon, and not consuming anything but water or juice during a full or new moon

- the Atkins diet—dieters cut out carbs almost entirely

- the Paleo diet—dieters eat only what people might have eaten in the Paleolithic era, which cuts out dairy and carbs

A nutritious diet combined with moderate exercise is the best way to lose weight and keep it off. A doctor can help create a healthy weight-loss plan.

These diets and others like them may be counterproductive to losing weight. "Fad diets generally rely on some trick to give the readers the appearance of novelty,"[54] researchers Dana K. Cassell and David H. Gleaves have noted. Commonly, a person's metabolism will slow down, causing one's body to react as though the dieter were starving. The body burns fewer calories and will frequently burn both fat and muscle. When the person quits dieting, they frequently gain weight more quickly as the body seeks to replace what it has lost while in starvation mode. In the worst-case scenario, dieting may even lead to eating disorders. Losing 1 to 2 pounds (0.5 to 0.9 kg) per week through healthy diet and exercise is a slower process, but it is easier to stick to and more likely to keep the weight off for good.

The Problems with BMI

Body mass index (BMI) is what most people use to calculate whether they are underweight, average, or overweight. However, BMI does not calculate how much of a person's weight is due to muscle, which weighs more than fat and is healthier. Nutritionist Angie Jaeger explains:

For example, a wrestler or heavy weight lifter can be inaccurately labeled overweight or obese due to the person's high muscle mass … The biggest problem with the BMI measure is that it does not take into consideration the differences between individuals, particularly lean body mass, [body type], age, and sex.[1]

BMI may be useful to give a general idea of a person's weight, but it should not be taken as the final word on whether or not someone is healthy. A doctor or nutritionist can do other tests to determine how accurate someone's BMI reading is.

1. Angie Jaeger, "BMI, Why?" Healthy Inclinations, July 18, 2016. hinclinations.wix.com/website#!BMI-why/yt080/578d0e850cf2779eabef9004.

Diet pills are another dangerous trend that play off of people's insecurities and desire to lose weight or build muscle fast without doing any hard work. The Food and Drug Administration (FDA) has warned against using them because some "are known to cause cancer. Others have been known to cause cardiac and pulmonary problems … Other supplements … have labels that don't accurately describe what FDA labs found in the ingredients."[55] Drugs such as ephedra and fen-phen have been banned for being harmful. The FDA does not regulate diet pills, which means anyone could make them and sell them without doing any kind of research on the side effects they may cause. Additionally, losing that much weight that quickly is very bad for the body, so if the pill works, it is harmful by definition. A balanced diet and moderate exercise is the best way to lose weight, keep it off, and feel more energized. To avoid frustration, journal about your progress: Weigh yourself once a week at the same time of day, and take note of things such as whether you feel happier, more energetic, stronger, and healthier.

Common Eating Disorders

According to the National Institute of Health, anorexia nervosa, bulimia nervosa, and binge eating disorder are considered mental disorders. People who have them are unable to stop their behavior, even though they often know it is unhealthy. Therapy is generally needed to help someone overcome his or her eating disorder. Accurate statistics about how many people have them are difficult to find because people generally try to keep it hidden. They know that friends and family would try to stop them from doing things related to their disorders, and they do not want to stop.

Anorexia is a very common eating disorder. People who have it think they are fat even when everyone around them can see that they are extremely thin. However, not everyone who is underweight has anorexia. Some people simply have trouble gaining weight because of their genetics. Similarly, not everyone who thinks he or she is fat has this disorder. The symptoms include "an intense fear of gaining weight, limiting calorie intake to as little as possible to maintain thinness, over-exercising, refusal to sustain a normal body weight, and a distorted view of one's body or weight, or denial of the dangers of one's low weight."[56] They are often proud of how much weight they have lost and are secretive about eating; they will try to avoid meals with people so no one can see how little they are eating.

People with bulimia do not starve themselves, but this does not mean they are healthier. Like those with anorexia, they have an intense fear of gaining weight and have a distorted view of their bodies, but they deal with it by eating a lot in one sitting—called bingeing—and then throwing up or using laxatives to get it out of their system quickly—called purging. People with one type of bulimia, called non-purging bulimia, will binge and then starve themselves for days afterward instead of throwing up. Signs of bulimia include "disappearance of large amounts of food, eating in secrecy, lack of control when eating, and frequent use of the bathroom after meals."[57] They can maintain a

Sufferers of bulimia often eat in secret and purge immediately afterward.

Eating Disorders and Abuse

Studies have shown that sexual abuse is linked to poor body image—between 30 and 60 percent of people treated for eating disorders have experienced sexual abuse at some point in their lives. People who were abused may no longer feel good about their body and may end up developing an eating disorder. Often this is because they are trying to control their body after an event where they had no control and are concerned with how other people are viewing their body. It is important for people who have been abused to remember that there is nothing wrong with their body and that they did not cause the assault to happen. Therapy for both the eating disorder and the assault is the key to helping people build up a positive self-image and overcome the pain of what happened to them.

normal body weight, unlike those with anorexia, but they suffer other health problems.

People with binge eating disorder eat massive portions of food at least once a week, but typically do not purge the way those with bulimia do. Frequently, binge eaters become overweight. "Compulsive overeaters are also overweight," writes Yancey, "but they may overeat all the time rather than binge."[58] Symptoms of binge eating include eating more food than is normal for a meal, eating large amounts even when not hungry, lack of control when bingeing, and feelings of shame and distress afterward. Binge eaters will often change their routines to make time for bingeing, hide the evidence of how much food they have eaten, and avoid eating meals with people.

These three eating disorders seem very different, but they have many similarities. They all have a lot to do with feelings of shame about the person's body and eating habits; they involve secretive behavior because the person knows others will disapprove of what they are doing; and they can all be deadly. Sufferers of anorexia may have a heart attack because the heart is weakened by the lack of nutrients. Sufferers of bulimia have tooth decay and problems with their throat because of the acid in their vomit. Binge eaters are at risk for diabetes and heart disease. Anyone who is suffering or knows someone who is

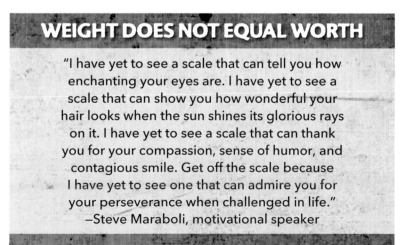

WEIGHT DOES NOT EQUAL WORTH

"I have yet to see a scale that can tell you how enchanting your eyes are. I have yet to see a scale that can show you how wonderful your hair looks when the sun shines its glorious rays on it. I have yet to see a scale that can thank you for your compassion, sense of humor, and contagious smile. Get off the scale because I have yet to see one that can admire you for your perseverance when challenged in life."
—Steve Maraboli, motivational speaker

Quoted in Shannon Butler, "20 Inspiring Quotes on Eating Disorder Recovery", Something for Kelly, February 4, 2014. somethingforkelly.org/20-inspiring-quotes-on-eating-disorder-recovery/

suffering with one of these conditions should tell a trusted adult and get help as soon as possible.

Over-Exercising and Bodybuilding

Broadly speaking, exercise covers a wide range of activities designed to improve health and fitness through physical activity. Because exercise and sports help burn fat calories, many people also exercise to lose weight or maintain a healthy weight. Likewise, exercise helps tone and shape the body, leading men and women to exercise for a better body image. Because bodies process calories more slowly as people grow older, exercise also balances the gradual weight gain that sometimes occurs as people reach middle age.

While exercise is generally thought of as positive and healthy, it can become an obsession. Exercise obsession leads to over-exercising and is often pursued to achieve a desired body shape and to enhance a body part (muscular arms, a flat stomach, etc.). Men and women who jog excessively, for instance, may damage knees or other body parts. "Too much exercise and the body breaks down physically," author Michelle Biton has written. "Bones suffer, as do tendons, ligaments, even muscles."[59] Exercise obsession is also common in people who have eating disorders: Exercise is used to burn off unwanted calories. "Breaking an exercise addiction can be as difficult as overcoming an eating disorder,"[60] Cassell and Gleaves have noted.

Bodybuilding is a type of exercise that involves lifting weights at home, school, or a health club. As with general exercise, bodybuilding is used to enhance body shape and self-esteem. Bodybuilding has generally been seen as a male-oriented sport, promoting more muscular body types. "Bodybuilding is becoming more and more popular worldwide as a way for men to attain the culturally valued slender, muscular body,"[61] Grogan stated. Over time, however, bodybuilding has also become more popular with women, though female bodybuilders may face social obstacles by attempting to achieve a body style that is less socially acceptable. "Bodybuilding is not generally seen as appropriate for women, and women who engage in this sport may

Women as well as men can be bodybuilders. Both are at risk for becoming obsessed and turning to steroid use to build more muscle.

face discrimination,"[62] Grogan noted. As with men, women have their own bodybuilding competitions.

Bodybuilding, like exercise in general, has a number of health benefits if practiced responsibly. When taken to extremes, however, bodybuilding may result in a number of unhealthy side effects. One particular danger has been the use of anabolic steroids to help build greater muscle mass. The use of steroids can have serious side effects, including liver damage, hypertension (high blood pressure), and kidney damage; also, the hypodermic needles that are frequently used by athletes to inject steroids may possibly spread infectious diseases such as HIV. Many of the side effects of steroids affect men and women differently. In women, steroids may cause baldness, breast reduction, the growth of body hair, and the deepening of voice; in men, steroids may cause infertility and the growth of breasts. For adolescents, the use of steroids may stunt the development of bone structure, especially if taken before a growth spurt.

Imagined Defects

While excessive dieting and exercise may represent a desire to alter one's overall body image, body dysmorphic disorder (BDD) focuses on an obsession with an imagined or mentally exaggerated body defect. It is common for those with BDD to focus on one or more body parts as unsatisfactory—typically the skin, hair, and the individual parts of the face; although any part of the body can be the cause of negative feelings. A person suffering from BDD may be distressed, and normal functioning may be impaired; he or she may believe that one of his or her body features is too big or too small, no matter how many times others tell them this is not true. BDD is estimated to occur in about 2 percent of the world's population and is equally common in women and men. Everyone has things about their body that they are unhappy with, but BDD has specific symptoms, such as:

- *Preoccupation with physical appearance*

- *Strong belief that you have an abnormality or defect in your appearance that makes you ugly*

- *Repeatedly examining yourself in the mirror*

- *Believing that others take special notice of your appearance in a negative way*

- *Frequent cosmetic procedures with little satisfaction*

- *Excessive grooming, such as hair plucking*

- *Feeling extremely self-conscious*

- *Refusing to appear in pictures*

- *Skin picking*

- *Comparing your appearance with that of others*

- *Avoiding social situations*

- *Wearing excessive makeup or clothing to camouflage perceived flaws*[63]

Muscle dysmorphia is a specific type of BDD that affects men more than women. Someone with muscle dysmorphia is obsessed with becoming more muscular and may be convinced that he is weak even if he has more muscles than the average man. This can lead to steroid abuse and over-exercise. Like eating disorders, BDD is most often developed in adolescence or young adulthood and may be accompanied by depression and social phobia, and in some cases it may include suicidal thoughts. People may think that sufferers of BDD are self-centered or vain, though the opposite is often true: People with BDD obsess about their appearance because they believe they are ugly.

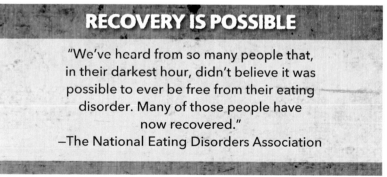

RECOVERY IS POSSIBLE

"We've heard from so many people that, in their darkest hour, didn't believe it was possible to ever be free from their eating disorder. Many of those people have now recovered."
—The National Eating Disorders Association

"Recovery," National Eating Disorders Association. www.nationaleatingdisorders.org/recovery.

Body Image Affects Emotions

Even if someone with a negative body image never develops one of these disorders, they may still suffer from anxiety about their appearance, low self-esteem, and depression. Talking to a thera-pist can be a helpful way to deal with these emotions, but there are also some things everyone can do in his or her daily life to help improve body image.

- Look at men and women you love, such as parents and friends. You probably think they are beauti-ful even though their bodies, like all bodies, have flaws. Remember that others feel the same way about you.

- Do not participate in body-shaming conversations, either about other people ("Becky wears way too much makeup.") or yourself, with friends ("I'm so fat."—"No you're not, I'm way fatter than you!"). Appearance is not a competition. You can tell someone he or she looks good without putting yourself or someone else down.

- When possible, try to eat healthy, get enough sleep, and exercise a moderate amount. Experts recom-mend nine hours of sleep per night and one hour of exercise per day.

- Replace negative thoughts with positive ones; if you find yourself thinking things such as, 'I'm ugly,' think instead of compliments you have received from others or things you like about yourself.

- Remember that bodies gain weight in response to stress or starvation. If you are under a lot of pres-sure at school or you have recently been on a crash diet, you may gain weight quickly as your body tries to protect itself. This is normal.

- Find or create an affirmation, which is a statement you can tell yourself to boost your self-esteem. Two examples are, "My appearance does not define my worth. I define my worth and I am worthy," and

"The only person I have to be better than is the person I was yesterday."

- Remember that you do not exist just to be attractive to someone else. You have other wonderful qualities to bring to the world.

- Remember that the media is lying when it tells you that you have to look a certain way in order to find love. In real life, people are attracted to all different kinds of body types and appearances, and if someone only wants you for your looks instead of your personality, he or she is not worth your time.

- Rely on your emotional support network. Talk to friends about your concerns in a body-positive way. Exercise together so you can motivate each other. However, be careful not to let encouragement cross over into shaming; do not start controlling what your friends eat or do. Ultimately, it is their choice, not yours.

- Remember that other people's choices are not an insult to your own choices. If someone says, "I want to be healthier," do not automatically think they mean, "You should be healthier."

- Remember that loving your body does not have to mean you do not want to make a change. You can love yourself and still want to lose weight, wear makeup, dye your hair, or get a tattoo. Loving yourself means remembering that you are a worthy person no matter what you look like.

CHAPTER 6

Body Modifications

Throughout history, body modifications, or body mods, have been seen as extreme, and the people who get them are often considered deviants, or people who do not fit into society. Some body mods are more accepted than others; for example, pierced ears have been around for thousands of years and are considered normal enough that people even get their babies' ears pierced sometimes. On the other hand, tattoos were seen for many years as something that only a criminal would get. They are still not entirely accepted in today's society, but now, many people no longer immediately assume that a person with tattoos is a bad person. In fact, 14 percent of Americans have at least one tattoo, and many have several.

Cosmetic surgery is another common way for people to change things about their appearance. These types of procedures include nose jobs, Botox, collagen injections to make lips look fuller, and face-lifts. Breast augmentations or reductions (making the breasts larger or smaller) are also common. However, cosmetic surgery can become an addiction, especially for people with BDD.

Piercings and tattoos show someone's personality and individuality, but only certain types of body mods are considered acceptable. These physical alterations, like dieting and exercise, have a lot to do with personal identity and body image development. In other cases, these acts may also be a form of rebellion.

Extreme Body Mods

Tattoos and body piercings once helped separate different subgroups from the mainstream, but today they are not considered very unusual. As tattoos and body piercing have become more popular in recent years in Western cultures, the shape and variety of procedures have increased. Piercings on ears, tongues, lips, noses, eyebrows, belly buttons, and nipples are all

Many of this man's body modifications are considered extreme by Western cultural standards.

common, and even more extreme piercings are now available. Piercing holes can be stretched by using plugs, and a corset piercing involves multiple piercings on the back, sides, or chest with string or ribbon pulled through them to look like the lacing of a corset. Some people get piercings all over their face and body. These types of piercings are not widely accepted in society yet.

Tattoos also fall into "acceptable" and "unacceptable" categories, according to our culture's standards. Some people think that no tattoos are acceptable and will falsely accuse people who get them of having loose morals or no common sense. Other people think only a few small tattoos or one large one are normal. Still others tattoo every inch of their bodies. The least accepted tattoos are on the face, especially ones that cover the whole face and make the person look like a skull, lizard, cat, or some other animal. In the past, many employers would not hire someone with tattoos or would require them to be covered at all times. As more and more people get them, many companies are changing these policies, but it is still a good idea to cover tattoos before a job interview.

Other forms of extreme body mods include surgery. People may split their tongues so they are forked like a snake's; create bumps in certain designs under the skin, which are known as dermal implants; get sharpened teeth implants; alter their eyes; make their ears pointed like an elf's; or engage in a process called scarification. Like a tattoo, scarification creates a permanent design on the skin, but instead of using colored ink, the design is scratched or burned onto the skin. "Some people don't want ink or foreign pigments in their body, like from tattoos," one scarification artist explained. "With scarification, the design is from your body only."[64]

Cosmetic Surgery

While tattoos and piercings decorate the body and enhance body image, they do not address concerns such as body weight and the effects of aging. Collagen, Botox, and liposuction, on the other hand, promise to make men and women thinner and reduce the effects of the aging process. All of these procedures

Rites of Passage

Most body mods in Western culture are done because people like the way they look and want to express their individuality. But in other cultures, they are a way to show that someone has passed from child to adult. For example, in Sudan, the Dinka tribe scarifies young adults' faces. The process lets children show their bravery in front of the tribe by not crying from the pain, and the scars let everyone know that this person is now an adult. Other tribes also use scarification, tattoos, and other forms of body modification as rites of passage.

are fairly new, dating back no further than the 1970s for collagen, the 1980s for liposuction, and the 1990s for Botox. All of these procedures have become extremely popular methods of enhancing body image.

The injected variety of collagen comes from cow skin, one of many products injected into the face to smooth wrinkles and to plump lips. The collagen is combined with an anesthetic (numbing medicine), mixed into a paste, and then injected into the desired area. An injection costs approximately $400 and lasts from two weeks to six months, at which time another injection is needed to achieve the same effect. Botox, which comes from a poisonous kind of bacteria, is used in a similar way. Botox works by paralyzing facial muscles that cause wrinkling, and the effects usually last between three and four months. Taken over a period of time, the effect of Botox may remain even without injections. In 2015, 2.4 million collagen injections and 6.7 million Botox injections were administered in the United States. These treatments can be dangerous if someone is allergic to them, and because Botox paralyzes the face, a person may have a difficult time making facial expressions until the treatment wears off.

Liposuction is a process by which plastic surgeons remove fat from beneath the skin. In 2015, 225,000 liposuction surgeries were performed. The procedure is popular with both men and women because it promises a quick fix for getting rid of

ULTRASOUND-ASSISTED LIPOSUCTION

Before

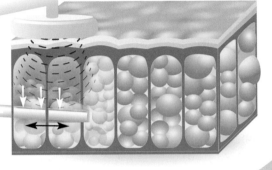

After

There are several different ways liposuction can be performed. In this one, ultrasound waves liquefy the fat before it is removed from under the skin.

fat. However, this surgery, like all surgeries, can have serious side effects such as infection, bumpy skin, or kidney problems. Additionally, if diet and exercise are not added to a person's life-style, he or she may need more than one liposuction treatment.

Breast augmentation is another common cosmetic surgery. In fact, the American Society of Plastic Surgeons reports that it has been the most popular surgery since 2006. In 2015, 279,000 people got implants to make their breasts larger.

Even as cosmetic surgery has become more common and accepted, and even as many people find it helpful, cosmetic surgery remains controversial for safety reasons. Silicone breast implants, for instance, sometimes rupture, which can lead to serious health problems. Also, poorly performed operations by unreliable surgeons are frequently reported. In the United States, the licensing of plastic surgeons is much less strict than for other types of doctors.

Gastric Banding Surgery

One kind of surgery that affects weight but is not considered cosmetic is gastric banding surgery, also called stomach stapling. It is only used in extreme cases—the only people who qualify are those who are very obese and who have already tried to lose weight with diet, exercise, and medication. It is not a cosmetic surgery because the point is not just to make someone thinner, but to eliminate the high blood pressure, diabetes, sleep apnea, and heart disease that many obese people suffer from. The surgery separates the stomach into two parts, "one of which is a very small pouch that can hold about one ounce of food."[1] People lose weight because they are no longer able to eat large amounts of food.

1. "Gastric Stapling (Restrictive) Surgery Procedure," Johns Hopkins Medicine. www.hopkinsmedicine.org/healthlibrary/test_procedures/gastroenterology/gastric_stapling_restrictive_surgery_procedure_92,p07989/.

Physically and Mentally Necessary Surgery

Reconstructive surgery is a type of surgery that is usually done to fix a health problem that also has an impact on body image. Reconstructive surgery is generally considered to be the opposite of cosmetic surgery—a necessity rather than only to improve appearance. Reconstructive surgery, the oldest type of plastic surgery, involves repairing bodies that have experienced trauma. "In World War II," Graydon explained, "soldiers were coming back from the European front with their faces so damaged that they were unrecognizable. Surgeons, in addition to trying to save their lives, did everything they could to patch up their faces."[65] Reconstructive surgery may also involve working with men and women who have had cancer, been in an accident, or had tumors removed. It is also commonly done on children who are born with a cleft lip or cleft palate, which is a split in the lip or roof of the mouth that can make it difficult for a child to eat and speak. This also gives their faces a more average appearance.

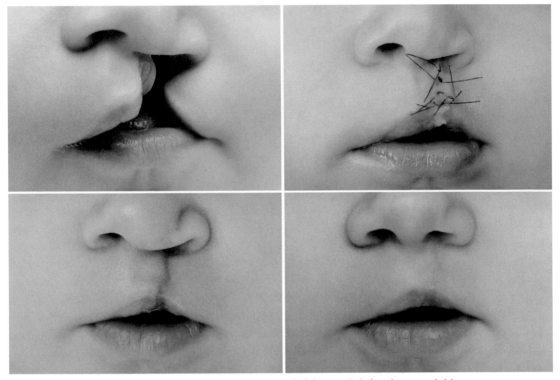

Reconstructive surgery is used to correct cleft lips and cleft palates in children.

COSMETIC SURGERY IS IRREVERSIBLE

"You only have one body, and once you change it through cosmetic surgery, things will never be the same again. You might think you've got nothing to lose, but surveys have shown that that's not always the sentiment you'll have after."

—Yagana Shah, associate editor for the *Huffington Post*

Yagana Shah, "4 Good Reasons To Never Get Plastic Surgery," *Huffington Post*, August 7, 2014. www.huffingtonpost.com/2014/08/07/cons-of-plastic-surgery_n_5618623.html.

A very basic benefit of reconstructive surgery revolves around self-image and body image. Although everyone's body changes over time, these changes are generally subtle, allowing the person to psychologically adjust to these changes. In the case of body trauma from war or surgery, however, the individual may find it difficult to adjust to sudden changes. Reconstructive surgery helps an individual adjust to these changes by making the body look more like it did before the trauma.

One common procedure is breast reconstruction, commonly performed after a mastectomy—the removal of part of or the entire breast, generally as a result of breast cancer. The surgeon forms a replacement from silicone or saline, and the reconstruction can sometimes be completed at the same time as the mastectomy. While many believe that breast implants can have a positive psychological impact leading to an improved body image, they also have several drawbacks. The reconstructed breast has no feeling, and it may need more surgery at a later date. Despite these drawbacks, a recent survey in the United States reported that the majority of women receiving the surgery were happy with the results. Recently, there has been a trend where women get a tattoo on top of or instead of a reconstructed breast. This is a way for them to cover the surgical scars and feel beautiful in their body again, although not everyone chooses to get one.

Breast reduction is another type of non-cosmetic procedure. This surgery is popular with women whose breasts are so large that they cause physical problems, such as back pain, and get in the way of them doing everyday activities, such as playing sports. Men may also choose to get a breast reduction if they have a condition called gynecomastia, a hormone imbalance that causes them to grow breasts. It is not uncommon for boys to develop this during puberty as their hormones are changing, and surgery is only recommended if they do not grow out of it or if their breasts are painful.

Surgery can have a positive impact on a person's life in specific situations, but it should not be taken lightly. Before considering cosmetic surgery, people should make a serious effort to love themselves in spite of their flaws. Everyone has things they dislike about their body, even people who have already had

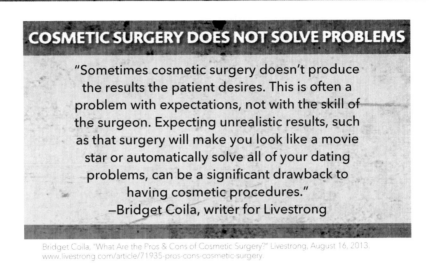

COSMETIC SURGERY DOES NOT SOLVE PROBLEMS

"Sometimes cosmetic surgery doesn't produce the results the patient desires. This is often a problem with expectations, not with the skill of the surgeon. Expecting unrealistic results, such as that surgery will make you look like a movie star or automatically solve all of your dating problems, can be a significant drawback to having cosmetic procedures."
—Bridget Coila, writer for Livestrong

Bridget Coila, "What Are the Pros & Cons of Cosmetic Surgery?" Livestrong, August 16, 2013. www.livestrong.com/article/71935-pros-cons-cosmetic-surgery.

cosmetic surgery. It is difficult not to, in a society that constantly pushes us to examine ourselves for flaws.

You Have the Power

Every day, no matter where we live, we see and hear things that influence our body image. At school, at home, online, and on TV, there are messages telling people what they "should" look like. Sometimes the messages come from a well-meaning friend or parent: "I just want you to be healthy," or "You have so much potential!" Other times, the comments are deliberately hurtful. Either way, the result is that people are left feeling as if they are worth less than someone who looks different than them.

It is impossible for people to control how others view them, but it is possible for everyone to learn to love his or her body as it is and try to ignore other people's negative comments. This is easier said than done—getting upset is a normal reaction, and it can be difficult to shake off an insult—but keeping a positive body image helps get over the pain of those insults more quickly. Two people can look very different, but both can be beautiful; there is no need for people to compare themselves when giving compliments or to tear others down for not looking a certain way.

The best way to change society's standards of beauty is to constantly challenge them. Give others body-positive compli-

A positive body image can contribute to high self-esteem and general satisfaction.

ments, especially on fashion choices that are out of the norm. Post positive things on social media. Support companies with models who are diverse in race, body type, and sexual orientation. Refuse to buy from companies whose ads make you feel bad about yourself. Challenge people when you hear them shame others. Cultural beauty standards are constantly changing, and you have the power to help shape them.

NOTES

Chapter 1: Understanding Body Image

1. Barbara Moe, *Understanding the Causes of a Negative Body Image*. New York, NY: Rosen, 1999, pp. 1–2.

2. Diane Yancey, *Eating Disorders*. Brookfield, CT: Twenty-First Century, 1999, pp. 58–59.

3. Michael P. Levine and Linda Smolak, "Body Image Development in Adolescence," *Body Image: A Handbook of Theory and Practice*, eds. Thomas Pruzinsky and Thomas F. Cash. New York, NY: Guilford, 2002, p. 77.

4. "Developing and Maintaining Positive Body Image," National Eating Disorders Association, July 14, 2016. www.nationaleatingdisorders.org/developing-and-maintaining-positive-body-image.

5. Joni E. Johnston, *Appearance Obsession: Learning to Love the Way We Look*. Deerfield Beach, FL: Health Communications, 1994, p. 23.

6. "Developing and Maintaining Positive Body Image."

7. Rachel Huxley and YangFeng Wu, "China Too Must Confront Obesity," SciDev, August 28, 2008. www.scidev.net/en/china/opinions/china-too-mustconfrontobesity.html.

8. Wang Ping, *Aching for Beauty: Footbinding in China*. New York, NY: Anchor, 2000, p. 3.

9. Ping, *Aching for Beauty*, p. ix.

10. Sarah Grogan, *Body Image: Understanding Body Dissatisfaction in Men, Women, and Children*. New York, NY: Routledge, 2008, p. 16.

11. Shari Graydon, *In Your Face: The Culture of Beauty and You*. Buffalo, NY: Annick, 2004, p. 24.

12. Barbara A. Cohen, "The Psychology of Ideal Body Image as an Oppressive Force in the Lives of Women," Center for Healing the Human Spirit, 1984. www.healingthehumanspirit.com /pages/body_img.htm.

13. Bob Batchelor, *The 1900s*. Westport, CT: Greenwood, 2002, p. 92.

14. Dorothy Hoobler and Thomas Hoobler, *Vanity Rules: A History of American Fashion & Beauty*. Brookfield, CT: Twenty-First Century, 2000, p. 112.

15. Hillel Schwartz, *Never Satisfied: The Cultural History of Diets, Fantasies and Fat*. New York, NY: Free Press, 1986, p. 336.

16. Gilda Marx, "The 90's Body—Toned over Thin as Ideal Body Type," *American Fitness*, January/February 1992.

Chapter 2: Body Image: Nature vs. Nurture

17. Adora Svitak, "The Asian Beauty Problem," *Huffington Post*, May 5, 2015. www.huffingtonpost.com/adora-svitak/teen-body-image_b_5251604.html.

18. Quoted in Svitak, "The Asian Beauty Problem."

19. Johnston, *Appearance Obsession*, p. 52.

20. Linda Smolak, "Body Image Development in Children," *Body Image: The Handbook of Theory, Research, and Clinical Practice*, eds. Thomas Pruzinsky and Thomas F. Cash. New York, NY: Guilford, 2002, p. 69.

21. Sunny Sea Gold, "Let's Talk About Our Moms and Our Body Issues," Greatist, February 24, 2016. greatist.com/live/body-image-issues-related-to-mothers.

22. "Research on Males and Eating Disorders." National Eating Disorders Association, www.nationaleatingdisorders.org/research-males-and-eating-disorders.

23. Tami L., e-mail interview by author. July 15, 2016.

24. Stacey Tantleff-Dunn and Jessica L. Gokee, "Interpersonal Influences on Body Image Development," *Body Image: The Handbook of Theory, Research, and Clinical Practice.* eds. Thomas Pruzinsky and Thomas F. Cash, New York, NY: Guilford, 2002, p. 110.

25. Andrea L. Meltzer and James K. McNulty, "Telling Women That Men Desire Women With Bodies Larger Than the Thin-Ideal Improves Women's Body Satisfaction," *Sage Journals*, December 10, 2014. spp.sagepub.com/content/6/4/391.

26. Luke Graham, "New Standards of Male Beauty Are Emerging in the Men's Cosmetics Sector," CNBC, January 28, 2016. www.cnbc.com/2016/01/28/new-standards-of-male-beauty-in-mens-cosmetics-sector.html.

27. BuzzFeed Video, "The Try Guys Get Photoshopped With Men's Ideal Body Types," YouTube, May 15, 2016. www.youtube.com/watch?v=dLNTb2zfh3Q.

28. Grogan, *Body Image*, pp. 150-51.

29. A. Kelly, e-mail interview by author. July 20, 2016.

30. A. Kelly, e-mail interview by author. July 20, 2016.

31. Ashley W., e-mail interview by author. July 28, 2016

Chapter 3: The Role of Media in Shaping Body Image

32. Brian Cuban, "Why It's Time to Stop Blaming the Media for Body Image Disorders," Greatist, April 9, 2014. greatist.com/happiness/media-male-body-image-eating-disorders.

33. Kate Fox, "Mirror, Mirror," Social Issues Research Centre, 1997. www.sirc.org/publik/mirror.html.

34. Brandon Keim, "The Media Assault on the Male Body," *Seed Magazine*, September 15, 2006. seedmagazine.com/news/2006/09/the_media_assault_on_male_body.php.

35. Johnston, *Appearance Obsession*, p. 18.

36. Kay Ireland, "How Do Actors Lose Weight So Fast?" Livestrong, October 21, 2013. www.livestrong.com/article/30807-actors-lose-weight-fast/.

37. Quoted in Erin Weinger, "Jennifer Lawrence on Her Dior Ads: 'Of Course It's Photoshop; People Don't Look Like That,'" *Hollywood Reporter*, February 28, 2013. www.hollywoodreporter.com/fash-track/jennifer-lawrence-her-photoshopped-dior-425504.

38. "How Many People Use Assistive Devices?" National Institute of Child Health and Human Development, November 30, 2012. www.nichd.nih.gov/health/topics/rehabtech/conditioninfo/Pages/people.aspx.

39. A. Kelly, e-mail interview by author. July 20, 2016.

40. Tina Fey, *Bossypants*. New York, NY: Little, Brown and Co., 2011, e-book.

41. Mindy Kaling, *Is Everyone Hanging Out Without Me? (and Other Concerns)*. New York, NY: Crown Archetype, 2011, e-book.

42. Buggheart, "The Mag for Plus Size Women Is Not Meaty Enough," Viewpoints, August 2008. www.viewpoints.com/Figure-Magazine-review-3af44.

Chapter 4: The Problem with Advertising

43. Dan Bilefsky, "Model in Gucci Ad Is Deemed 'Unhealthily Thin' by British Regulator," *New York Times*, April 06, 2016. www.nytimes.com/2016/04/07/business/international/gucci-ad-unhealthily-thin-model.html?_r=0.

44. Alissa Quart, *Branded: The Buying and Selling of Teenagers.* New York, NY: Perseus, 2003, p. xvi.

45. Michelle Lee, *Fashion Victim: Our Love-Hate Relationship with Dressing, Shopping, and the Cost of Style.* New York, NY: Broadway, 2003, p. 46.

46. Ian Halperin, *Bad and Beautiful: Inside the Dazzling and Deadly World of Supermodels.* New York, NY: Citadel, 2001, p. 203.

47. BuzzFeed Video, "The Try Guys Get Photoshopped With Men's Ideal Body Types."

48. BuzzFeed Video, "The Try Guys Get Photoshopped Like Women," YouTube, July 12, 2016. www.youtube.com/watch?v=2Zw634ZZiek.

49. Janday Wilson, "Making My Natural Hair Look 'Acceptable' Takes Up An Obscene Amount of My Time," XOJane, June 3, 2013. www.xojane.com/beauty/natural-hair-twist-out.

50. Cited in Susan L. Bryant, "The Beauty Ideal: The Effects of European Standards of Beauty on Black Women," *Columbia Social Work Review*, vol. IV, 2013, p. 85. cswr.columbia.edu/article/the-beauty-ideal-the-effects-of-european-standards-of-beauty-on-black-women/.

Chapter 5: Consequences of Poor Body Image

51. Johnston, *Appearance Obsession*, pp. 17–18.

52. Saul McLeod, "Low Self Esteem," Simply Psychology, 2012. www.simplypsychology.org/self-esteem.html.

53. Kay Uzoma, "Percentage of Americans Who Diet Every Year," Livestrong, June 24, 2015. www.livestrong.com/article/308667-percentage-of-americans-who-diet-every-year/.

54. Dana K. Cassell and David H. Gleaves, *The Encyclopedia of Obesity and Eating Disorders*. New York, NY: Facts On File, 2000, p. 91.

55. Lorne Fultonberg, "FDA Warns of 'Dangerous' Weight Loss, Body-building Pills Available in Oklahoma," News Channel KFOR, May 17, 2016. kfor.com/2016/05/17/fda-warns-of-dangerous-weight-loss-body-building-pills-available-in-oklahoma/.

56. "Anorexia Nervosa," Helpguide.org, August 2009. helpguide.org/mental/anorexia_signs_symptoms_causes_treatment.htm.

57. Jacquelyn Eckern, "Bulimia Nervosa: Causes, Symptoms, Signs & Treatment Help," Eating Disorder Hope RSS, November 9, 2015. www.eatingdisorderhope.com/information/bulimia.

58. Yancey, *Eating Disorders*, p. 24.

59. Michelle Biton, "Are You Exercise Obsessed?", *alive*, February 1, 2009. www.alive.com/1482a4a2.php?subject_bread_cramb=6.

60. Cassell and Gleaves, *The Encyclopedia of Obesity and Eating Disorders*, p. 88.

61. Grogan, *Body Image*, p. 95.

62. Grogan, *Body Image*, p. 63.

63. "Body Dysmorphic Disorder," Mayo Clinic, February 2, 2009. www.mayoclinic.com/health/bodydysmorphic disorder/DS00559/DSECTION=symptoms.

Chapter 6: Body Modifications

64. Quoted in Erica Lenti, "People Paying to Have Their Skin Cut, Etched, Burned or Branded as Scarification Gains Popularity," *National Post*, October 14, 2013. news.nationalpost.com/news/canada/people-paying-to-have-their-skin-cut-etched-burned-or-branded-as-scarification-gains-popularity.

65. Graydon, *In Your Face*, p. 59.

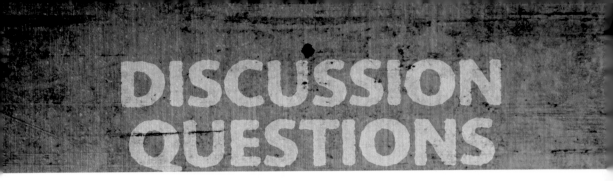

Chapter 1: Understanding Body Image

1. How do you feel about your own body image?
2. How has the "ideal" body type changed over time?
3. What is the difference between positive and negative body image?

Chapter 2: Body Image: Nature vs. Nurture

1. How is the development of body image affected by biology?
2. In what ways do family and peers affect body image?
3. Does gender influence the development of body image issues?
4. Which do you think has a bigger impact on body image: nature or nurture?

Chapter 3: The Role of Media in Shaping Body Image

1. Is your idea of the "ideal" body type the same as or different than what the media shows?
2. Besides the ones listed in this chapter, what are some other groups that are ignored in the media?
3. What are some TV shows and movies that celebrate different body types? What are some that mock different body types?
4. How has social media changed the way you view body image?

Chapter 4: The Problem with Advertising

1. What are some examples of advertisements that show an unrealistic body type?

2. How have ads affected your personal body image?

3. How has advertising affected your view of what is beautiful?

Chapter 5: Consequences of Poor Body Image

1. What are some of the dangers of crash or fad diets?

2. What are some healthy diet and exercise routines?

3. What are some ways you can help improve body image for yourself and your friends?

Chapter 6: Body Modifications

1. What is your opinion of tattoos and piercings? Has it changed over time? If so, how?

2. What are the differences and similarities between reconstructive and cosmetic surgery?

3. What motivates most people to seek out cosmetic surgery?

About-Face
P.O. Box 191145
San Francisco, CA 94119
Phone: (415) 839-6779
Website: www.about-face.org
About-Face is a nonprofit organization that holds workshops in the San Francisco Bay area aimed at improving self-esteem and body image for girls and women by giving them resources to identify and challenge harmful messages from advertising and the media. Its website features a "Gallery of Offenders" and "Gallery of Winners" showing the worst and best portrayals of body image in ads and encouraging people to ask questions about what the ads are showing and how they make the viewer feel. Although the program is mostly targeted at women, they welcome male participants as well. Their website states that 35 percent of workshop participants are young men.

Black Girls Rock!
57 West 57th Street, 4th Floor
New York, NY 10019
Phone: (888) 895-3974
E-mail (general info): info@blackgirlsrockinc.com
E-mail (youth programs): programs@blackgirlsrock.org
E-mail (volunteer inquiries): volunteer@blackgirlsrock.org
Website: www.blackgirlsrockinc.com
Black Girls Rock! is a nonprofit organization that aims to provide support for young women of color through mentoring and volunteer work, and to encourage analysis of the ways women of color are shown in the media. They run a yearly leadership conference and a summer Queens Camp where girls of color can connect with each other and with mentors.

National Association of Anorexia and Associated Disorders (ANAD)

750 East Diehl Road #127
Naperville, IL 60563
Phone: (630) 577-1333
E-mail: anadhelp@anad.org
Website: www.anad.org

ANAD offers hotline counseling, operates an international network of support groups for people with eating disorders and their families, and provides referrals to health care professionals who treat eating disorders. It produces a quarterly newsletter and information packets and organizes national conferences and local programs. All ANAD services are provided free of charge.

7 Cups of Tea

Website: www.7cups.com

Using the app or the website, people can reach out to an anonymous listener to discuss problems both big and small. The listeners do not judge, solve problems, or give advice; they affirm emotions and give users a safe place to vent their feelings. There are also peer chat rooms and resources that help people find a licensed therapist, either online or in their area.

Society for Adolescent Health and Medicine (SAHM)

1 Parkview Plaza, Suite 800
Oakbrook Terrace, IL 60181
Phone: (847) 686-2246
Website: www.adolescenthealth.org

SAHM is a multidisciplinary organization of professionals committed to improving the physical and psychosocial health and wellbeing of all adolescents. It helps plan and coordinate national and international professional education programs on adolescent health. Its publications include the monthly Journal of Adolescent Health and the quarterly SAHM Newsletter.

Books

Fletcher, Carrie Hope. *All I Know Now*. London, UK: Sphere, 2015.
Carrie Hope Fletcher has a top-rated YouTube channel where she posts videos about the knowledge she has gained on the road to adulthood. That knowledge and advice is collected in this book to give teens and preteens a guide to navigating the pitfalls of young adulthood.

Ford, Jean. *No Quick Fix: Fad Diets & Weight-Loss Miracles*. Broomall, PA: Mason Crest, 2015.
There are many diets and pills out there that promise fast, easy weight loss with little to no effort. Unfortunately, they either do not work or work too well, with unhealthy consequences for the body. This book discusses the traps the diet industry sets up and how to avoid them.

Libal, Autumn. *Health Implications of Cosmetic Surgery, Make-overs, and Body Alterations*. Philadelphia, PA: Mason Crest Publishers, 2014.
This book discusses the risks that come with cosmetic surgery and the trap of wanting a makeover to change everything that a person is unhappy about in his or her life. It discusses America's obsession with beauty and offers ways to be happy based more on personality than looks.

Nagle, Jeanne. *Why People Get Tattoos and Other Body Art*. New York, NY: Rosen Publishing, 2012.
This book examines the reasons why people in cultures around the world choose to get decorative body art. The discussion

includes the cultural, religious, and aesthetic reasons for getting tattoos and piercings presented in an objective voice, showing both sides of the argument so readers can form their own opinions.

Rissman, Rebecca. *Asking Questions About Body Image in Advertising*. Mankato, MN: Cherry Lake Publishing, 2016.
This book provides an in-depth look at the ways advertisers change bodies to make them more appealing to consumers, giving readers the tools they need to spot the tricks that are designed to make them feel bad about their body.

Taylor, Julia V. *The Body Image Workbook for Teens: Activities to Help Girls Develop a Healthy Body in an Image-Obsessed World*. Oakland, CA: Instant Help Books, 2014.
This workbook provides exercises to help girls navigate topics such as comparison, negative self-talk, toxic friendships, perfectionism, and more. It teaches coping mechanisms and helps girls understand why they feel the way the do about certain issues.

Websites

BMI Project
www.kateharding.net/bmi-illustrated
Blogger Kate Harding created a slideshow on Flickr from user-submitted photos that show how inaccurate BMI is as an indicator of health.

Eating Disorder Hope
www.eatingdisorderhope.com
This website offers articles about various eating disorders such as anorexia, bulimia, and food addiction, with information about the disorders and ways to overcome them. It includes information on different types of therapy and a directory to find licensed treatment centers and therapists.

Girls' Health

www.girlshealth.gov

Healthy eating tips and information about weight loss are provided so girls can make the best choices about their meals. The site includes articles about how to make healthy food choices as a vegetarian, with food allergies, and at restaurants.

Health-Calc

www.health-calc.com

This site provides several different calculators to give a more accurate measurement of overall health. In addition to a BMI calculator, there are calculators to assess total energy expenditure, ideal body weight, weight loss based on calories, waist to height ratio, percentage of body fat, and more. These can be used to determine current fitness and plan a healthy weight-loss program if necessary. However, this site is not a substitute for a doctor.

Live Science

www.livescience.com

A search for "body image" provides many articles discussing the scientific research behind our culture's obsession with beauty. Some topics include disproving the myth that overweight people lack self-control, how much of a role genetics play in our satisfaction with our bodies, and ways to improve body image.

National Eating Disorders Association

www.nationaleatingdisorders.org

NEDA provides education and resources for those affected by eating disorders. The organization campaigns for increased funding for research and treatment related to eating disorders. NEDA also serves as a clearinghouse for information on eating disorders and partners with various organizations to facilitate this purpose.

Proud2BMe

proud2bme.org

Built for young adults, this site offers a variety of ways to build confidence and body positivity. It includes advice columns, articles about body positivity, forums where teens can discuss issues, and information about eating disorders, mental illness, ethical makeup companies, healthy recipes, and much more.

TeensHealth

kidshealth.org/teen

TeensHealth provides educational information and advice for teenagers. It is a nonprofit organization and features a qualified staff of health professionals. Articles cover multiple body image issues from self-esteem to body piercings.

INDEX

A

Aching for Beauty (Wang), 18
advertising
    beauty contests and, 56
    corset, 20
    entertainment and, 54
    targeting children/
      adolescents, 56–57
    use of sex in, 55
Advertising Standards Author-
    ity, 54
age/aging, 8, 20–21, 25, 36,
    39, 46, 60–61, 74, 82–83
American Fitness (magazine),
    23
American Society of Plastic
    Surgeons, 84
anorexia, 6, 31, 43, 71, 73
Atkins diet, 69

B

Barbie dolls, 57
Batchelor, Bob, 20
beauty standards
    for boys, 32–36
    for girls, 32–34, 36
    LGBT community,
      36–38, 50, 55
    set by fashion industry,
      61–64

binge eating disorder, 6, 40,
    65, 71, 73
Biton, Michelle, 74
blood type diet, 68
body art. *see also* body pierc-
    ing; tattoos
body dysmorphic disorder
    (BDD), 76–77, 80
body image
    age and, 60, 82–83
    biological influences on,
      24–27
    cultural customs/
      traditions and, 14–18,
      83
    definition of, 6
    feedback from
      family/friends and, 27
    health and, 38–40
    how to improve, 78–79
    influences shaping,
      8–10, 31–32
    negative, 13
    parents' impact on
      children's, 27–30
    positive, 12
    self-image vs., 12
    shifting ideas about,
      10–11, 14–23
    use in advertising,
      33–34, 45–47

body mass index (BMI), 66, 70

body modification
    dermal implants, 7, 82
    piercings, 6–7, 80–82
    scarification, 82–83
    surgery, 7, 27, 46, 59, 65, 80, 82–88
    tattoos, 6–7, 79–83, 87

body piercing, 6–8, 80–82

bodybuilding, 74–76

Bossypants (Fey), 51

Botox, 7, 25, 80, 82–83

Boys' Life (magazine), 56

boys/men
    anorexia in, 6
    body image concerns of, 6–8, 32–33, 35–38, 41–43, 55, 74
    breast reduction for, 87

brand names, 47

breast
    augmentation, 27, 80, 84
    reconstruction, 87
    reduction, male, 87

Brumberg, Joan Jacobs, 43

bulimia, 6, 71–73

C

"Campaign for Real Beauty," 33–34

cancer, 61–62, 70, 85, 87

Captain America: The First Avenger (movie), 41–42

cartoons, 41, 43

Cassell, Dana K., 69, 74

Centers for Disease Control and Prevention, 48

children/adolescents
    marketing products to, 56–57
    prevalence of obesity among, 67

China, 15–18

cleanse, 68

clothes, 11, 21, 25–26, 28, 36, 47, 54, 57, 58–59, 77

Cohen, Barbara A., 20

collagen, 80, 82–83

comic books, 41

corset
    dangers of, 18
    piercing, 7, 82
    waist training, 18, 20–21

cosmetic surgery, 7, 27, 46, 59, 65, 80, 82–88

Cosmo Girl (magazine), 56

Cosmopolitan (magazine), 21

crash diet, 65, 67–68, 78

D

Derenne, Jennifer L., 46

detox, 68

dieting
    children and, 7
    dangers of, 67–71
    obsession with, 6, 67

Dior, 47

direct comments, 25, 27–31, 38–39, 44, 55, 62, 88

Dove Soap, 33–34

E

eating disorders. *see also* an-
    orexia; binge eating disor-
    der; bulimia
exercise, 6, 18, 23–24, 28, 33,
    68–69, 70, 74–80, 84–85

F

fashion magazines, 21, 46,
    51–52, 58, 63
fashion models, 16, 21–23,
    33, 35, 46, 48, 50–52,
    54–55, 58–59, 60–64, 90
Fey, Tina, 51
flappers, 21
Food and Drug Administra-
    tion (FDA), 70
foot-binding, in China, 16–18
Fox, Kate, 45

G

gastric banding surgery, 85
genes, 8, 24–25, 27, 40
Gibson, Charles Dana, 20
Gibson girl, 20–21
Gibson man, 21
Girls' Life (magazine), 56
girls/women
        body image concerns of,
            32–34, 36–38
        dieting and, 7, 23
Gleaves, David H., 69, 74
Gokee, Jessica L., 32
Graydon, Shari
        on reconstructive
            surgery, 85
        on Rubens' women, 19

Grogan, Sarah
    on aging in men vs.
        women, 36
    on beauty standards, 19
    on bodybuilding, 74–75
Gucci, 54

H

Halperin, Ian, 59
Hatfield, Elaine, 23
Hawkeye Initiative, The (web-
    site), 41
Hoobler, Dorothy, 21
Hoobler, Thomas, 21
Huffington Post, 18, 25, 86
Huxley, Rachel, 15

J

Johnston, Joni E., 13, 27, 46,
    65
Jones, Georgina, 15

K

Kaling, Mindy, 51
Keim, Brandon, 46

L

Ladies' Home Journal (maga-
    zine), 20
Lawrence, Jennifer, 47
Lee, Michelle, 58
Levine, Michael P., 12
liposuction, 7, 46, 59, 82–84
lunar diet, 69

M

magazines
    advertising, 43, 47, 54,
        56, 58, 63
    fashion, 20–21, 46,
        51–52, 58, 63
    models, 11, 21, 45–46,
        50–52, 58–59, 63
    plus-size, 51–52, 63
    young adult, 56
Maraboli, Steve, 73
Marx, Gilda, 23
McCarthy, Melissa, 44
media
    conflicting messages by,
        52–53
    consumption of, 43
    eating disorders and,
        54–55
    presents distorted view
        of society, 45–47
    scapegoat for social
        problems, 50–52
    underrepresentation of
        minorities in, 48–50
MH-18 (magazine), 56
Miss America pageant, 56
modeling (concept), 27, 32,
    41, 50
Moe, Barbara, 11

N

National Eating Disorders
    Association (NEDA),
    12–13, 30, 77
National Institute of Health,
    71

New York Times, 54
1900s, The (Batchelor), 20
No Body's Perfect (Kirberger),
    14

O

obesity/overweight, epidemic
    of, 66–67
obsession
    with dieting, 6, 67
    with exercise, 6, 23, 33,
        71, 74–77

P

Paleo diet, 69
parents, 25, 27–32, 46, 57,
    78, 88
peer pressure, 32
Photoshop, 35, 46–47, 52,
    54, 59–60
Ping, Wang, 17–18
plastic surgery. *see also* cos-
    metic surgery; reconstruc-
    tive surgery
plus-size models, 51–52,
    58–59, 63

Q

Quart, Alissa, 56

R

raw food diet, 68
reconstructive surgery, 85–87
Rubens, Helene, 19
Rubens, Peter Paul, 19

S

scarification, 82–83

Schumer, Amy, 41

Schwartz, Hillel, 23

self-esteem, 7, 10, 12–13, 33, 36, 43, 47, 57, 65, 74, 78, 89

self-image, 9–10, 12, 26, 28, 30, 33–34, 38, 40, 43, 47–48, 63, 72, 87

Seventeen (magazine), 56

shaming

body, 6, 31, 39, 44–45, 65, 78–79

fat, 6, 25, 29–30, 39, 41, 43, 63, 78

ways to respond to, 44

Smolak, Linda, 12, 27–28

Social Issues Research Centre, 45

social media, 44, 52, 63, 88

society, 7, 10, 17, 20, 30, 33, 35–36, 46, 50–51, 61, 63, 65, 80, 82, 88

Sports Illustrated (magazine), 56, 63

Sports Illustrated Kids (magazine), 56

Sprecher, Susan, 23

steroids, anabolic, 6, 33, 38, 52, 55, 65, 75–77

Stuart, Madeline, 63–64

Svitak, Adora, 25

T

Tantleff-Dunn, Stacey, 32

Target stores, 26, 57

tattoos, 6–7, 79–83, 87

teasing, 7, 27, 32, 41

Teen Vogue (magazine), 56

"This Girl Can," 63–64

Try Guys, 35, 59

Twiggy, 21–23

V

vanity sizing, 57

Viewpoints (website), 52

W

Western culture, 9, 12, 16, 43, 65, 80–81, 83

World Health Organization (WHO), 66

Wu, YangFeng, 15

Y

Yancey, Diane, 11, 30, 73

PICTURE CREDITS

Cover Jan H. Andersen/Shutterstock.com; p. 7 (girl cartoon) Pensiri/
Shutterstock.com; p. 8 Tristan Savatier/Moment/Getty Images; p. 11
SpeedKingz/Shutterstock.com; p. 13 Justin Sullivan/Getty Images;
p. 17 Print Collector/Hulton Archive/Getty Images; p. 19 Barney Burstein/
Corbis Historical/Getty Images; p. 22 Lisa Maree Williams/Getty Images
Entertainment/Getty Images; p. 24 Kletr/Shutterstock.com; p. 26 Brasil2/
E+/Getty Images; p. 28 wavebreakmedia/Shutterstock.com; p. 29
Gladskikh Tatiana/Shutterstock.com; p. 34 Mike Albans/NY Daily News
via Getty Images; p. 35 Istvan Csak/Shutterstock.com; p. 37 CREATISTA/
Shutterstock.com; p. 42 Atlaspix/Alamy Stock Photo; p. 45 (left) Nadya
Korobkova/Shutterstock.com; p. 45 (right) Ysbrand Cosijn/
Shutterstock.com; p. 47 BAKOUNINE/Shutterstock.com; p. 49 Cultura
Limited/Superstock.com; p. 51 Helga Esteb/Shutterstock.com; p. 58
paultarasenko/Shutterstock.com; p. 60 Iulian Valentin/Shutterstock.com;
p. 62 Charlotte Purdy/Shutterstock.com; p. 64 Arun Nevader/Getty Images
for Art Hearts Fashion; p. 66 sunsinger/Shutterstock.com; p. 69 udra11/
Shutterstock.com; p. 72 Photographee.eu/Shutterstock.com; p. 75 chaoss/
Shutterstock.com; p. 81 MENAHEM KAHANA/AFP/Getty Images; p. 84
Designua/Shutterstock.com; p. 86 malost/Shutterstock.com; p. 89 iordani/
Shutterstock.com.

ABOUT THE AUTHOR

Meghan Green has edited a number of books for young people on the topics of social justice and self-esteem. She also occasionally gives talks at local schools on these topics. She is a social worker who specializes in working with developmentally disabled individuals. Meghan lives in Pennsylvania with her husband, Kris. She still occasionally struggles with her body image, but she tries to focus on the things she likes about herself more than the things she doesn't.